They Can't Pull Us Up: Harriet Tubman and Her Life

Danita Smith

Copyright © 2016 Danita Smith

Red and Black Ink, LLC

All rights reserved.

No part of this publication may be reproduced, stored in a retrieval system, or transmitted by any means, electronic mechanical photocopying, recording, or otherwise without written permission from the copyright owner and publisher.

ISBN: 0-9971386-8-8
ISBN-13: 978-0-9971386-8-9

DEDICATION

This book is dedicated to our children and our future.

Notes

Our goal is to uplift children through education and history and to promote positive images of ourselves and others.

Please look out for more of our titles,

Stories about Black History!

Also visit our website,

BlackandEducation.com.

CONTENTS

    Notes

1	The Backdrop for Her Life	Pg 1
2	Social and Moral/Religious Support for Slavery	Pg 19
3	Political Actions That Supported the Existence of Slavery	Pg 51
4	The Place Where Harriet Tubman Was Born	Pg 73
5	Solemn Resolution	Pg 101
6	Harriet's Parents, Other Heroes and the Dover Eight	Pg 127
7	Harpers Ferry and Troy, NY	Pg 147
8	From Questions of this Class Spring all Our Constitutional Controversies	Pg 155
9	Gullah Islands, Intelligence and the Civil War	Pg 183
10	The First Woman in American Military History	Pg 201
11	We're Rooted	Pg 213
	Appendix: Final Thoughts	Pg 221
	References and Photos by Chapter	Pg 223

iv

Chapter 1:

The Backdrop for Her Life

To get an understanding of the types of things Harriet Tubman did with her life, it's important to understand the system of slavery into which she was born.

There was economic, political, social and so-called "moral" support for slavery throughout the Western Hemisphere from about 1500 to the late 1800s.

The Economic Support for Slavery and Greed

Simply put, Africans were chained and brought to South America, Central America, the Caribbean and North America to do work for the economic benefit of other people. Denmark, the Netherlands, France, Sweden, Spain, Portugal and England all participated in slavery in the Western Hemisphere.[1] Their efforts began in the 1500s and 1600s and lasted through parts of the 1800s, with Brazil being the last country in the Western Hemisphere to abolish slavery in 1888.[2]

---

[1] Danish National Archives. "The Danish Slave Trade—Timeline for Teaching Purposes," Rigsarkivet. Accessed 8-2016.

Reuters. "In-Depth, Chronology: Who banned slavery when? March 22, 2007." http://www.reuters.com/article/uk-slavery-idUSL1561464920070322

[2] Hebrard, Jean. "Slavery in Brazil: Brazilian Scholars in the Key Interpretive Debates." University of Michigan Center for Latin and Caribbean Studies. Vol. 1, 2013.

It was not easy to clear land, build buildings, set up cities and to establish thousands of acres of land upon which to produce crops (i.e., sugar cane, tobacco, cotton, etc.) that would become staples in many of the economies of the Western Hemisphere and throughout many countries in Europe. The number of human beings taken from Africa far outweighed the number of European settlers who journeyed across the Atlantic ocean, from about 1500 to 1820—certain studies have estimated the ratio of Africans to Europeans, during that time, to be at least 4:1.[3]

While it is true that sugar cane and tobacco were early crops that propelled South American, Caribbean and North American settlements into economic viability, by no means were the people who were enslaved forced to do only agricultural work.

---

[3] David Eltis. "A Brief Overview of the Trans-Atlantic Slave Trade." Voyages: The Trans-Atlantic Slave Trade Database. Accessed May 3, 2016. http://www.slavevoyages.org/assessment/essays#

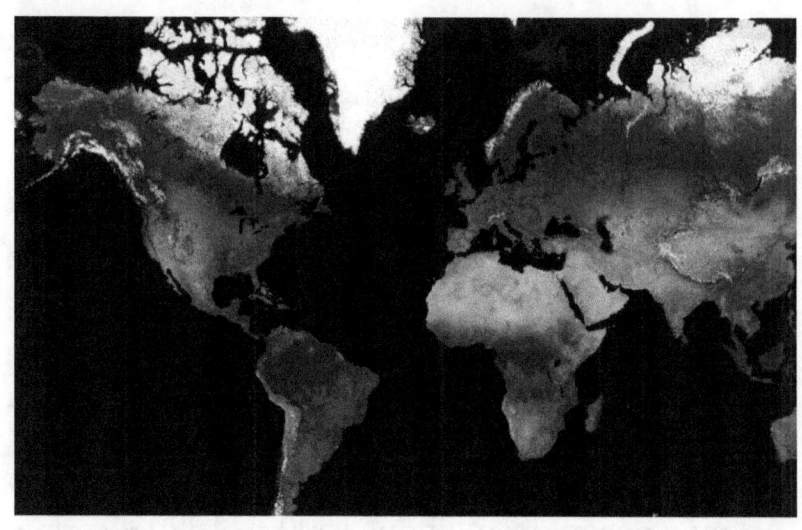

As mentioned, land needed to be cleared, buildings needed to be erected and the foundations needed to be laid for many of the societies that were developing in the Western Hemisphere, at that time. It was not uncommon to find enslaved people completing construction projects, clearing out land, building canals, loading and unloading docks, doing agricultural work, working in small businesses, building ships, etc., in addition to doing domestic work and other forms of labor.

For example, in colonial New York enslaved workers were present in as many as 41% of the city's households.[4] They built the wall that Wall Street is named after, they built the first city hall, constructed the city's hospital, built docks, roads, churches, Fort Amsterdam, and much of the city's infrastructure.[5]

In fact, a separate burial ground was set aside for Africans (free and enslaved), which was used from about the 1690s to 1794. It was located in, what is today, Lower Manhattan and was accidentally unearthed in 1991 during the construction of a Federal office building.[6]

New York City, 2014.

---

[4] New York Historical Society. "Slavery in New York." Accessed April 2015. http://www.slaveryinnewyork.org/history.htm.

[5] Ibid.

[6] General Services Administration: The African Burial Ground. "GSA and the African Burial Ground." Accessed April 2015.

In short, enslaved men and women did whatever type of work was required of them.

Lower Manhattan, 2010.

There was not only economic value in having an enslaved workforce and in the goods their labor produced, there was also a value in the slaves themselves. Included in the ownership of human beings was the ability to buy and sell them in open markets throughout the many areas where slavery existed. This meant that a human being could be sold, relatively easily, and that having them conferred a certain amount of status onto an owner—just like having a piece of property.

On the eve of the Civil War, there were about

four million enslaved men, women and children in the United States, alone. The business of selling and trading human beings was a very real and sordid part of the economics of slavery. If you added up the monetary value of the men, women and children who were enslaved in the United State, alone, just prior to the start of the Civil War, it would add up to be well over a billion dollars—**over a billion dollars** in terms of money at that time!

When you consider that the United States purchased the entire expanse of the Louisiana Purchase in 1803 for $15 million, any group of "goods" valued at well over a billion dollars in the 1800s was not an insignificant part of an economy and when you factor in the other types of businesses that supported slavery, it helps you understand that it was a major force, hidden and seen, throughout various parts of the economy in the United States.[7] Trading in slaves not only attracted businesses that dealt directly in selling human beings, but it also attracted businesses that supported and/or conducted transactions with

---

[7] U.S. Department of State, Office of the Historian. "Milestones 1801-1829: Louisiana Purchase, 1803." Accessed Nov. 2016. https://history.state.gov/milestones/1801-1829/louisiana-purchase

slave holders—blacksmiths, merchants, shipbuilders, factory owners, gun manufacturers, bankers, farmers, etc.

Cotton Became "King"

Thus, many industries were intertwined with slavery, but nowhere was this more evident than in the production, trade and manufacturing of products made from cotton. Cotton became a major part of the textile industry.

Now, if you are going to manufacture different types of fabric, you need the raw materials to do it. By the mid 1800s the United States was "growing 75% of the world's supply of cotton" and the American South accounted for **60% of the country's exports**—"most of it in cotton."[8]

This growth was supported by textile mills which sprung up in New England and in Great Britain in the very late 1700s and by new machines that spun and wove cotton….and of course by the invention of the cotton gin.

---

[8] National Archives and Records Administration. "Teaching with Documents: Eli Whitney's Patent for the Cotton Gin." Accessed May 2015.

Cotton Gin

In 1792 Eli Whitney left Massachusetts to head south. Whitney had recently graduated from Yale and was in debt. Instead of practicing law, he decided to get a job—he accepted a job as a tutor in Georgia. He was to be the tutor for the children of a southern slave owner on a plantation.

When he arrived he found that plantations there were experiencing a decline in the quality of their soil due to tobacco and other products that had been grown in it for years. A neighbor, Catharine Greene, who was the widow of the famous Revolutionary War general, Nathanael Greene, encouraged Eli Whitney to come work on her plantation to help find a solution for the challenges they were facing.[9]

Long-staple cotton could only be grown along the coast and short-staple cotton, which was grown in this area, had sticky green seeds throughout it which had to be hand-picked and cleaned. This was labor-intensive, thus Eli Whitney worked on and created a machine to

---

[9] Williams, Arden. "Catharine Greene (1755 - 1814)." *New Georgia Encyclopedia.* Georgia Humanities Council. Accessed May 2015.

separate seeds from cotton fiber. It became the first device (outside of human hands) to clean short-staple cotton—it could process up to fifty pounds of clean cotton in a day and, ironically, it was created on a slave plantation.

Whitney received the patent for the cotton gin in 1794 and, given the simultaneous development of factories and cotton mills, the demand for cotton grew. The yield of cotton, thus, doubled in each decade after 1800…after the invention of the cotton gin.[10] The impact this had on slavery was dramatic. The number of human beings needed to harvest and produce this raw material rose sharply. In his 1853 book, Solomon Northup described what it was like for him to grow cotton in Louisiana.

> "…inasmuch as some may read this book who have never seen a cotton field, a description of the manner of its culture may not be out of place.
>
> The ground is prepared by throwing up beds or ridges, with the plough— back-furrowing, it is called. Oxen and

---

[10] National Archives and Records Administration. "Teaching with Documents: Eli Whitney's Patent for the Cotton Gin." Accessed May 2015.

mules, the latter almost exclusively, are used in ploughing. The women as frequently as the men perform this labor, feeding, currying, and taking care of their teams, and in all respects doing the field and stable work, precisely as do the ploughboys of the North.

The beds, or ridges, are six feet wide, that is, from water furrow to water furrow. A plough drawn by one mule is then run along the top of the ridge or center of the bed, making the drill, into which a girl usually drops the seed, which she carries in a bag hung round her neck. Behind her comes a mule and harrow, covering up the seed, so that two mules, three slaves, a plough and harrow, are employed in planting a row of cotton. This is done in the months of March and April. Corn is planted in February. When there are no cold rains, the cotton usually makes its appearance in a week. In the course of eight or ten days afterwards the first hoeing is commenced. This is performed in part, also, by the aid of the plough and mule. The plough passes as near as possible to the cotton on both sides, throwing the furrow from it. Slaves follow with their hoes, cutting up the grass and cotton, leaving hills two feet and a half apart. This is called scraping cotton. In two weeks more commences the second hoeing. This time the furrow is thrown towards the cotton. Only one stalk, the largest, is now left standing in each hill. In another fortnight it is hoed the third time, throwing the furrow towards the cotton in the same manner as before, and killing all the grass between the rows. About the first of July, when it is a foot high or thereabouts, it is hoed the fourth and last time. Now the whole space between the rows is ploughed, leaving a deep water furrow in the center. During all these hoeings the overseer or driver follows the slaves on horseback with a whip, such as has been described. The fastest hoer takes the lead row. He is usually about a rod in advance of his companions. If one of them passes him, he is whipped. If one falls behind or is a moment idle, he is whipped. In fact, the lash is flying from morning until night, the whole day long. The hoeing season thus continues from April until July, a field having no sooner been finished once, than it is commenced again.

In the latter part of August begins the cotton picking season. At this time each slave is presented with a sack. A strap is fastened to it, which goes over the neck, holding the mouth of the sack breast high, while the bottom reaches nearly to the ground. Each one is also presented with a large basket that will hold about two barrels. This is to put the cotton in when the sack is filled. The baskets are carried to the field and placed at the beginning of the rows.

When a new hand, one unaccustomed to the business, is sent for the first time into the field, he is whipped up smartly, and made for that day to pick as fast as he can possibly. At night it is weighed, so that his capability in cotton picking is known. He must bring in the same weight each night following. If it falls short, it is considered evidence that he has been laggard, and a greater or less number of lashes is the penalty.

An ordinary day's work is two hundred pounds. A slave who is accustomed to picking, is punished, if he or she brings in a less quantity than that. There is a great difference among them as regards this kind of labor. Some of them seem to have a natural knack, or quickness, which enables them to pick with great celerity, and with both hands, while others, with whatever practice or industry, are utterly unable to come up to the ordinary standard. Such hands are taken from the cotton field and employed in other business. Patsey, of whom I shall have more to say, was known as the most remarkable cotton picker on Bayou Bœuf. She picked with both hands and with such surprising rapidity, that five hundred pounds a day was not unusual for her.

The hands are required to be in the cotton field as soon as it is light in the morning, and, with the exception of ten or fifteen minutes, which is given them at noon to swallow their allowance of cold bacon, they are not permitted to be a moment idle until it is too dark to see, and when the moon is full, they often times labor till the middle of the night. They do not dare to stop even at dinner time, nor return to the quarters, however late it be, until the order to halt is given by the driver.

The day's work over in the field, the baskets are 'toted,' or in other words, carried to the gin-house, where the cotton is weighed. No matter how fatigued and weary he may be—no matter how much he longs for sleep and rest—a slave never approaches the gin-house with his basket of cotton but with fear. If it falls short in weight—if he has not performed the full task appointed him, he knows that he must suffer… So, whether he has too little or too much, his approach to the gin-house is always with, fear and trembling. Most frequently they have too little, and therefore it is they are not anxious to leave the field. After weighing, follow the whippings; and then the baskets are carried to the cotton house, and their contents stored away like hay, all hands being sent in to tramp it down. If the cotton is not dry, instead of taking it to the gin-house at once, it is laid upon platforms, two feet high, and some three times as wide, covered with boards or planks, with narrow walks running between them."[11]

This was the kind of work that was done to supply the world with 75% of its cotton and which made the United States of America the world's largest supplier of cotton in the mid 1800s.

---

[11] Northup, Solomon. *Twelve Years a Slave: Narrative of Solomon Northup, a Citizen of New York, Kidnapped in Washington City in 1841, and Rescued in 1853, from a Cotton Plantation Near the Red River, in Louisiana.* Auburn: Derby & Miller, 1853.

Chapter 2:

Social and Moral/ Religious Support for Slavery

Were Americans really ready to live in a society that was free and equal for everyone, in the 1600s,

1700s or 1800s? The short answer to that is, "No, not everyone was really ready for a society like that." There were many people who simply did not believe that the proclamations made in the Declaration of Independence or in the Constitution applied to black people or to their descendants. It is difficult to express it in words, but the sentiments shared by Senator Jefferson Davis, of Mississippi, during his final address to Congress (to announce the secession of Mississippi from the Union before the Civil War) give you an idea of what he, and others who felt like him, believed as it relates to the equality of the races.

> "It has been a conviction of pressing necessity, it has been a belief that we are to be deprived in the Union of the rights which our fathers bequeathed to us, which has brought Mississippi into her present decision. She has heard proclaimed the theory that all men are created free and equal, and this made the basis of an attack upon her social institutions; and the sacred Declaration of Independence has been invoked to maintain the position

of the equality of the races. That Declaration of Independence is to be construed by the circumstances and purposes for which it was made. The communities were declaring their independence; the people of those communities were asserting that no man was born—to use the language of Mr. Jefferson—booted and spurred to ride over the rest of mankind; that men were created equal—meaning the men of the political community; that there was no divine right to rule; that no man inherited the right to govern; that there were no classes by which power and place descended to families, but that all stations were equally within the grasp of each member of the body-politic. These were the great principles they announced; these were the purposes for which they made their declaration; these were the ends to which their enunciation was directed. **They have no reference to the slave**; else, how happened it that among the items of arraignment made against George III was that he endeavored to do just what the North has endeavoring of late to do—to stir up insurrection among our slaves? Had the Declaration announced that the negroes were free and equal, how was the Prince to be arraigned for stirring up insurrection among them? And how was this to be enumerated among the high crimes which caused the colonies to sever their connection with the mother country? When our Constitution was formed, the same idea was rendered more palpable, for there we find provision made for that very class of persons as **property; they were not put upon the footing of equality with white men—not even upon that of paupers and convicts; but, so far as representation was concerned, were discriminated against as a lower caste, only to be represented in the numerical proportion of three fifths.**

Then, Senators, we recur to the compact which binds us together; we recur to the principles upon which our Government was founded; and when you deny them, and when you deny to us the right to withdraw from a Government which thus perverted threatens to be destructive of our rights, we but tread in the path of our fathers when we proclaim our independence, and take the hazard. This is done not in hostility to others, not to injure any section of the country, not even for our own pecuniary benefit; but from the high and solemn motive of defending and protecting the rights we inherited, and which it is our sacred duty to transmit unshorn to our children."[12]

- Jefferson Davis, January 21, 1861

Jefferson Davis equated enslaving human beings with the rights granted to states by the

---

[12] U.S. Congressional Documents and Debates, 1774 - 1875 *Congressional Globe*, Senate, 36th Congress, 2nd Session, pg. 487.

Constitution and he wrapped his stance that people could be held as property in a misguided cloud of defending rights which should be passed on to "our children."

Jefferson Davis reaffirmed his support for slavery and his beliefs about black people in his role as President of the Confederate States of America and in his address to the Confederate Congress, in April of 1861; referring to the condition of slavery under which black people had been subjected:

> "In moral and social condition they had been elevated from brutal savages into docile, intelligent, and civilized agricultural laborers, and supplied not only with bodily comforts but with careful religious instruction."[13]
>
> - Jefferson Davis, April 29, 1861

He was not alone in his beliefs about black people…other congressmen, presidents, supreme court justices, and many ordinary people also shared these views.

---

[13] Richardson, James Daniel. *A Compilation of the Messages and Papers of the Confederacy.* Nashville: United States Publishing Company, 1905, pg. 68.

Moral, Political and Social Issues

There were people who came down on opposite sides of the argument around whether slavery was right—which is crazy to even think about…that there were many people who actively supported the existence of slavery.

Anthony Burns, 1855.[14]

We will delve into one specific case that demonstrated the clash of social, moral and

---

[14] Anthony Burns / drawn by Barry from a daguereotype [sic] by Whipple & Black ; John Andrews, engraver. Boston : R.M. Edwards, printer, c1855.

political views surrounding slavery and that sparked an outcry across the country; this was the case of Anthony Burns. (There were many other contentious cases, as well).

On May 24, 1854,[15] Anthony Burns was walking down a street in Boston, when a man came up behind him and put his hand on his shoulder. The man made him wait for a minute and said, "You are the man who broke into the silversmith's shop the other night!" Anthony Burns assured him that he had the wrong person, but before he could even finish his sentences, six or seven men came up behind him and lifted him off of his feet.

They took Burns to the courthouse, where he waited for sometime. The silversmith never showed up to accuse Burns and he was never given anymore information, until a door opened. Charles Suttle walked through the door and said, "How do you do, Mr. Burns?" He asked Burns if there would be any trouble with him taking Burns back to Virginia. You see, in March of that year Anthony Burns escaped from slavery in Virginia and made his way to Boston. Burns subsequently

---

[15] Stevens, Charles Emery. *Anthony Burns: A History.* Boston: John P. Jewett and Company, 1856.

wrote a letter to his brother...who was still enslaved by Suttle. The letter was written in Boston, but mailed from Canada to conceal Burns' location. Suttle intercepted the letter, figured out where Burns was staying and came to Boston to claim him under the Fugitive Slave Act of 1850.[16]

Anthony Burns could do nothing...he felt it was inevitable that he would be returned to slavery. On May 25, 1854, a trial (or hearing) was conducted to hear the facts of Suttle's claim. A lawyer, by the name of Dana, stepped up on Burns' behalf and convinced the commissioner to postpone the hearing for a few days.

This gave time for the people of Massachusetts to react. Over ten years earlier, 65,000 people petitioned the state's government to pass laws restricting state authorities from participating in the capture of fugitive slaves and prohibiting escaped slaves from being housed in state facilities, so as to have "the effect of forever separating the people of Massachusetts from all connection with

---

[16] See also, "Anthony Burns in New York", "Ransom of Burns". *The Liberator.* Garrison, William Lloyd, March 9, 1855.

slavery."[17] So, many people felt that the capture of Anthony Burns was in violation of the laws of Massachusetts and that it was contrary to the will of the people of Massachusetts.

On the evening of May 26th two public meetings were held—one with mostly white attendees, at Faneuil Hall, and one with mostly African-American attendees, at Tremont Temple. At Faneuil Hall many citizens argued that they wanted to live and die in a land of true liberty....for all...not just liberty for a few.

At Tremont Temple, the meeting was shorter. The people there decided to go down to the courthouse and liberate Burns, by force.

As word got out that people were gathering at the courthouse, the numbers grew. A group of African-American and white men picked up a beam and used it to pound against the door of the courthouse. The authorities inside were prepared and they repelled the attempted entry.

That night was a very contentious evening in Boston, but the people in the streets were never

---

[17] Joint Special Committee of the Senate and House of Representatives of the State of Massachusetts on the Petition of George Latimer and Others. House, No. 41, Commonwealth of Massachusetts, General Court, 1843.

able to take Anthony Burns from the courthouse. Over the ensuing days the hearing would take place. President Franklin Pierce called in marines and artillery to protect the courthouse and to guard city streets. The commissioner ruled in favor of Charles Suttle and Anthony Burns was officially going to be returned to slavery.

The courtroom was then cleared and Burns was prepared for transportation. Some 50,000 people lined the streets of Boston; shouting their disapproval. Burns was escorted by federal troops, through the streets of the city, to a U. S. revenue cutter (ship)...for transportation back to Virginia.

Once he arrived in Norfolk, there were people gathered to see the man who had been called the "Boston Lion" and many people followed behind him in the streets as he was taken to the local jail. Burns had been captured and returned to slavery at a cost of thousands and thousands of dollars to the U. S. government.

He was kept in jail for two days in Norfolk, then he was transferred to a slave trader's jail in Richmond. The jail served as a place where enslaved men and women were held, while waiting to be sold in Richmond. It was also a place where a slave owner could house a person as punishment. Burns was held in a tiny cell, on the upper floor, for four months...while being shackled for a good deal of that time (the iron cuffs he was placed in caused him scars that he would carry for the rest of his life). He was eventually sold to a man, named David McDaniel, from North Carolina.

McDaniel was a planter (of cotton), a slave-trader and a horse-dealer. He often sold the men and women he owned, but kept them busy growing cotton until offers for them were made. He also kept a harem of enslaved women, from amongst which he was not averse to selling them or the children he bore with them, to prospective buyers.

McDaniel put Anthony Burns in charge of his stable and also instructed him to carry his wife wherever she needed to go. After being there for a relatively short period of time, Burns one day took McDaniel's wife to a neighbor's house. While there, someone recognized him and said he was the man who had caused all of that commotion with his capture in Massachusetts. The daughter of this neighbor heard this and subsequently wrote a letter to her sister, who was in Massachusetts. This sister mentioned this fact, while at a social function, and a reverend who knew Burns overheard it. He immediately wrote a letter to David McDaniel, asking him to sell Burns. McDaniel agreed, for a price of $1,300. Reverend Leonard Grimes, an African-American minister, was told of the deal and he agreed to lead the charge. Rev. Grimes told every one of the baptist ministers he knew and even pastors from other denominations.

Leonard Grimes was the pastor of the Twelfth Baptist Church. Before coming to Boston, Grimes ran a hackman/ taxi business in Washington, D.C. He used his business to secretly escort escaped slaves. In 1839, he was arrested and sentenced to two years of hard labor in the Richmond Penitentiary and fined $100, for helping a woman and her children escape from Virginia.

Upon his release, he made his way to Boston and became minister of the Twelfth Baptist Church. Dozens of escaped slaves were a part of his congregation and his church became known as "The Fugitive Slave Church."

Grimes was only able to raise $600 through his efforts to help Burns, while a meeting had been arranged with McDaniel for February 27, 1855. The meeting was to take place in Baltimore and, as the date approached, Grimes did not have enough money...but he would not give up!

He was able to get a loan, from a Boston banker, who took the $600 that was collected and loaned Grimes the rest of the money. So, Rev. Grimes had the $1,300 and he made his way to Baltimore.

Meanwhile, McDaniel took Anthony Burns to Norfolk via a train. The word had gotten out, through a close friend, that McDaniel was trying to sell Burns, which would give him his freedom. Passengers on the train became irate and the conductor said he would never have let McDaniel on the train if he had known what was going on. Once they got to Norfolk, they headed straight to a boat. While on the boat, Anthony Burns was recognized and surrounded by angry white citizens. They demanded that McDaniel not give in to the North. McDaniel rebuffed the crowd and, at one point, pulled his pistol. He promised that if anything went wrong, he wouldn't sell Burns and would bring him back, but said that he was going to go keep the deal. The boat was delayed, but it eventually took off. McDaniel arrived in Baltimore two hours late.

When they all arrived at the hotel, Anthony Burns was excited to see Rev. Grimes. Burns said, "I knew if this was going to take place, Leonard Grimes would be at the bottom of it!"

Grimes presented McDaniel with the check, but McDaniel refused to accept it—he wanted cash. Rev. Grimes had to go to a local bank to cash the check, but the bank would not cash a check for anyone who was from out of town, unless someone from Baltimore vouched for that person. Grimes did not know anyone in Baltimore and he was stuck, again, in a difficult situation.

Finally, the owner of the hotel, where the meeting had been held, agreed to vouch for Grimes...and the money was given to McDaniel. Anthony Burns was then a free man! He made his way back north and received much attention and notice because of the entire ordeal. According to his autobiography, he was asked by "Barnum" to come to New York to tell his story on stage, in front of a live audience, for five weeks. Burns summarily refused, indicating that he would be displayed like a "monkey" if he agreed to do such a show.

Burns, instead, pursued his life-long desire to become a preacher and, with the help of a woman from Massachusetts, he attended college at Oberlin in Ohio. When he secured his path forward, he wrote to the church he attended while in slavery (he was allowed to join a church) in Virginia to ask for a note of dismission and recommendation so that he could join another church in the North. He never received a reply directly, but he did receive a copy of the *Front Royal Gazette*, dated November 8, 1855, in which an open response from his church was printed.

> "Whereas, Anthony Burns, a member of this church, has made application to us, by a letter to our pastor, for a letter of dismission, in fellowship, in order that he may unite with another

church of the same faith and order; and whereas, it has been satisfactorily established before us, that the said Anthony Burns absconded from the service of his master, and refused to return voluntarily—thereby disobeying both the laws of God and man; although he subsequently obtained his freedom by purchase, yet we have now to consider him only a *fugitive from labor* (as he was before his arrest and restoration to his master), have therefore,

"*Resolved*, Unanimously, that he be excommunicated from the communion and fellowship of this church.

"Done by order of the church, in regular meeting, this twentieth day of October, 1855.[18]

Wm. W. West, Clerk

---

[18] Stevens, Charles Emery. *Anthony Burns: A History.* Boston: John P. Jewett and Company, 1856.

His church viewed his fight for freedom as "disobeying the laws of God and man." This view was not unusual, as people had selfishly used the Bible to support the existence of slavery for many years (e.g., Leviticus 25: 44 - 46).

This case showed the extent to which the federal government was willing to go to uphold the Fugitive Slave Act; through the use of the military. It also demonstrated the increase in the opposition to slavery in the form of tens of thousands of people demonstrating in the streets of Boston. It illustrated the types of conflicts that could arise when people could be forcibly taken back into slavery and it showed that some people could equate searching for freedom with violation of the laws of God.

Anthony Burns later moved to St. Catharines, Canada in 1860 and became the pastor of Zion Baptist Church.[19] He died in 1862 and is buried there. St. Catharines is the same area of Canada where Harriet Tubman settled when she brought her family and others to freedom there.

---

[19] St. Catharines Museum, Museum Chat. "Salem Chapel, BME Church and Zion Baptist Church." February 9, 2016. https://stcatharinesmuseumblog.com/2016/02/09/salem-chapel-bme-church-and-zion-baptist-church/. Accessed September 28, 2016.

A Voice Crying Out in the Wilderness

There were many people who began to be highly vocal about their opposition to slavery, but there was no argument more powerful than the argument that came from the mouth of someone who had been subjected to the injustice of slavery.

There were people who argued that slavery brought Christianity to African people; that the horrors talked about relative to slavery were exaggerations and not true; that God granted people the right to own slaves in the Bible; that slaves would be disconsolate and unhappy if they were given the awesome responsibilities of freedom; and that the Constitution supported slavery, therefore, it should be legally upheld!

Frederick Douglass famously summed up a response to many of these arguments in a speech he gave during a Fourth of July celebration, on July 5, 1852.

> "Fellow-Citizens—Pardon me, and allow me to ask, why am I called upon to speak here to-day? What have I, or those I represent, to do with your national independence? Are the great principles of political freedom and of natural justice, embodied in that Declaration of Independence, extended to us? and am I, therefore, called upon to bring our humble offering to the national altar, and to confess the benefits, and express devout gratitude for the blessings, resulting from your independence to us?
>
> Would to God, both for your sakes and ours, that an affirmative answer could be truthfully returned to these questions! Then would my task be light, and my burden easy and delightful. For who is there so cold

that a nation's sympathy could not warm him? Who so obdurate and dead to the claims of gratitude, that would not thankfully acknowledge such priceless benefits? Who so stolid and selfish, that would not give his voice to swell the hallelujahs of a nation's jubilee, when the chains of servitude had been torn from his limbs? I am not that man. In a case like that, the dumb might eloquently speak, and the 'lame man leap as an hart.'

But, such is not the state of the case. I say it with a sad sense of the disparity between us. I am not included within the pale of this glorious anniversary! Your high independence only reveals the immeasurable distance between us. The blessings in which you this day rejoice, are not enjoyed in common. The rich inheritance of justice, liberty, prosperity, and independence, bequeathed by your fathers, is shared by you, not by me. The sunlight that brought life and healing to you, has brought stripes and death to me. This Fourth of July is yours, not mine. You may rejoice, I must mourn. To drag a man in fetters into the grand illuminated temple of liberty, and call upon him to join you in joyous anthems, were inhuman mockery and sacrilegious irony. Do you mean, citizens, to mock me, by asking me to speak to-day? If so, there is a parallel to your conduct. And let me warn you that it is dangerous to copy the example of a nation whose crimes, towering up to heaven, were thrown down by the breath of the Almighty, burying that nation in irrecoverable ruin! I can to-day take up the plaintive lament of a peeled and woe-smitten people.

'By the rivers of Babylon, there we sat down. Yea! we wept when we remembered Zion. We hanged our harps upon the willows in the midst thereof. For there, they that carried us away captive, required of us a song; and they who wasted us required of us mirth, saying, Sing us one of the songs of Zion. How can we sing the Lord's song in a strange land? If I forget thee, O Jerusalem, let my right hand forget her cunning. If I do not remember thee, let my tongue cleave to the roof of my mouth.'

Fellow-citizens, above your national, tumultous joy, I hear the mournful wail of millions, whose chains, heavy and grievous yesterday, are to-day rendered more intolerable by the jubilant shouts that reach them. If I do forget, if I do not faithfully remember those bleeding children of sorrow this day, 'may my right hand forget her cunning, and may my tongue cleave to the roof of my mouth!' To forget them, to pass lightly over their wrongs, and to chime in with the popular theme, would be treason most scandalous and shocking, and would make me a reproach before God and the world. My subject, then, fellow-citizens, is AMERICAN SLAVERY. I shall see this day and its popular characteristics from the slave's point of view. Standing there, identified with the American bondman, making his wrongs mine, I do not hesitate to declare, with all my soul, that the character and conduct of this nation never looked blacker to me than on this Fourth of July. Whether we turn to the declarations of the past, or to the professions of the present, the conduct of the nation seems equally hideous and revolting. America is false to the past, false to the present, and solemnly binds herself to be false to the future. Standing with God and the crushed and bleeding slave on this occasion, I will, in the name of humanity which is outraged, in the name of liberty which is fettered, in the name of the constitution and the bible, which are disregarded and trampled upon, dare to call in question and to denounce, with all the emphasis I can command, everything that serves to perpetuate slavery—the great sin and shame of America! 'I will not equivocate; I will not excuse;' I will use the severest language I can command; and yet not one word shall escape me that any man, whose judgment is not blinded by prejudice, or who is not at heart a slaveholder, shall not confess to be right and just.

But I fancy I hear some one of my audience say, it is just in this circumstance that you and your brother abolitionists fail to make a favorable impression on the public mind. Would you argue more, and denounce less, would you persuade more and rebuke less, your cause would be much more likely to succeed. But, I submit, where all is plain there is nothing to be argued. What point in the anti-slavery creed would you have me argue? On what branch of the subject do the people of this country need light? Must I undertake to prove that the slave is a man? That point is conceded already. Nobody doubts it. The slaveholders themselves acknowledge it in the enactment of laws for their government. They acknowledge it when they punish disobedience on the part of the slave. There are seventy-two crimes in the state of Virginia, which, if committed by a black man (no matter how ignorant he be), subject him to the punishment of death; while only two of these same crimes will subject a white man to the like punishment. What is this but the acknowledgement that the slave is a moral, intellectual, and responsible being. The manhood of the slave is conceded. It is admitted in the fact that southern statute books are covered with enactments forbidding, under severe fines and penalties, the teaching of the slave to read or write. When you can point to any such laws, in reference to the beasts of the field, then I may consent to argue the manhood of the slave. When the dogs in your streets, when the fowls of the air, when the cattle on your hills, when the fish of the sea, and the reptiles that crawl, shall be unable to distinguish the slave from a brute, then will I argue with you that the slave is a man!

For the present, it is enough to affirm the equal manhood of the Negro race. Is it not astonishing that, while we are plowing, planting, and reaping, using all kinds of mechanical tools, erecting houses, constructing bridges, building ships, working in metals of brass, iron, copper, silver, and gold; that, while we are reading, writing, and cyphering, acting as clerks, merchants, and secretaries, having among us lawyers, doctors, ministers, poets, authors, editors, orators, and teachers; that, while we are engaged in all manner of enterprises common to other men—digging gold in California, capturing the whale in the Pacific, feeding sheep and cattle on the hillside, living, moving, acting, thinking, planning, living in families as husbands, wives, and children, and, above all, confessing and worshiping the Christian's God, and looking hopefully for life and immortality beyond the grave—we are called upon to prove that we are men!

Would you have me argue that man is entitled to liberty? that he is the rightful owner of his own body? You have already declared it. Must I argue the wrongfulness of slavery? Is that a question for republicans? Is it to be settled by the rules of logic and argumentation, as a matter beset with great difficulty, involving a doubtful application of the principle of justice, hard to be understood? How should I look to-day in the presence of Americans, dividing and subdividing a discourse, to show that men have a natural right to freedom, speaking of it relatively and positively, negatively and affirmatively? To do so, would be to make myself ridiculous, and to offer an insult to your understanding. There is not a man beneath the canopy of heaven that does not know that slavery **is wrong for him.**

What! am I to argue that it is wrong to make men brutes, to rob them of their liberty, to work them without wages, to keep them ignorant of their relations to their fellow-men, to beat them with sticks, to flay their flesh with the lash, to load their limbs with irons, to hunt them with dogs, to sell them at auction, to sunder their families, to knock out their teeth, to burn their flesh, to starve them into obedience and submission to their masters? Must I argue that a system, thus marked with blood and stained with pollution, is wrong? No; I will not. I have better employment for my time and strength than such arguments would imply.

What, then, remains to be argued? Is it that slavery is not divine; that God did not establish it; that our doctors of divinity are mistaken? There is blasphemy in the thought. That which is inhuman cannot be divine. Who can reason on such a proposition! They that can, may! I cannot. The time for such argument is past.

At a time like this, scorching irony, not convincing argument, is needed. Oh! had I the ability, and could I reach the nation's ear, I would to-day pour out a fiery stream of biting ridicule, blasting reproach, withering sarcasm, and stern rebuke. For it is not light that is needed, but fire; it is not the gentle shower, but thunder. We need the storm, the whirlwind, and the earthquake. The feeling of the nation must be quickened; the conscience of the nation must be roused; the propriety of the nation must be startled; the hypocrisy of the nation must be exposed; and its crimes against God and man must be proclaimed and denounced.

What to the American slave is your Fourth of July? I answer, a day that reveals to him, more than all other days in the year, the gross injustice and cruelty to which he is the constant victim. To him, your celebration is a sham; your boasted liberty, an unholy license; your national greatness, swelling vanity; your sounds of rejoicing are empty and heartless; your denunciations of tyrants, brass-fronted impudence; your shouts of liberty and equality, hollow mockery; your prayers and hymns, your sermons and thanksgivings, with all your religious parade and solemnity, are to him mere bombast, fraud, deception, impiety, and hypocrisy—a thin veil to cover up crimes which would disgrace a nation of savages. There is not a nation on the earth guilty of practices more shocking and bloody, than are the people of these United States, at this very hour.

Go where you may, search where you will, roam through all the monarchies and despotisms of the old world, travel through South America, search out every abuse, and when you have found the last, lay your facts by the side of the every-day practices of this nation, and you will say with me, that, for revolting barbarity and shameless hypocrisy, America reigns without a rival."[20]

---

[20] Douglass, Frederick. *My Bondage and My Freedom.* 1855.

Chapter 3:

Political Actions That Supported the Existence of Slavery

There were men and women who did not want to socialize with black people, some who thought that slavery was good for Africans, and others who benefited, economically, from the existence of slavery…but the legal support for slavery was founded in the Constitution.

Article I, Section 2: Representatives and direct Taxes shall be apportioned among the several States which may be included in the Union, according to their respective Numbers, which shall be determined by adding the whole Number of free Persons, including those bound to Service for a Term of Years, and excluding Indians not taxed, three fifths of all other Persons.

Article I, Section 9: The Migration or Importation of such Persons as any of the States now existing shall think proper to admit, shall not be prohibited by the Congress prior to the Year one thousand eight hundred and eight, but a Tax or duty may be imposed on such Importation, not exceeding ten dollars for each Person.

Article IV, Section 2: No person held to Service or Labour in one State, under the Laws thereof, escaping to another, shall, in Consequence of any Law or Regulation therein, be discharged from such Service or Labour, but shall be delivered up on Claim of the Party to whom such Service or Labour may be due.

10th Amendment: The powers not delegated to the United States by the Constitution, nor prohibited by it to the States, are reserved to the States respectively, or to the people.

These passages provided the legal support for slavery that many states felt they needed; they were also the basis for many acts of congress that would later become law.

For example, the Constitution was the basis for the 1793 Fugitive Slave Law, which was signed by George Washington (in support of Article IV, Section 2), and the importation of enslaved men and women into the United States did not become illegal until January 1, 1808 (due to the instructions given in Article I, Section 9).

From the perspective of the millions of people who were enslaved, it was clear that the country was going to put the interests of slaveholders before the rights and interests of the many men, women and children who were enslaved.

In 1820, approximately two years before Harriet Tubman's birth, the nation was dealing with the issue of expansion. Missouri requested to be admitted into the Union, in late 1819 (as a state with slavery). At the time, there was a balance between states with slavery and states who had already abolished (or were in the process of abolishing) slavery. So, to admit Missouri into the Union would upset the balance of power in national politics.

This was no easy matter to resolve and in 1820 the country settled on a compromise.

Senator Henry Clay would become known as the "Great Compromiser," as he famously brokered a deal that would allow Missouri to be admitted as a slave state and Maine to be admitted as a free state—keeping the balance of power equal between the number of slave and free states in the country. He also put forth a solution for future admissions; an imaginary line would be drawn across the country that would prevent slavery from existing above the 36 degree, 30 minute latitude line (with the exception of Missouri).[21]

> "SEC. 8. And be it further enacted. That in all that territory ceded by France to the United States, under the name of Louisiana, which lies north of thirty-six degrees and thirty minutes north latitude, not included within the limits of the state, contemplated by this act, slavery and involuntary servitude, otherwise than in the punishment of crimes, whereof the parties shall have been duly convicted, shall be, and is hereby, forever prohibited: Provided always, That any person escaping into the same, from whom labour or service is lawfully claimed, in any state or territory of the United States, such fugitive may be lawfully reclaimed

---

[21] Library of Congress. Primary Documents in American History. "Missouri Compromise."

and conveyed to the person claiming his or her labour or service as aforesaid."[22]

You can see that the language from Article IV, Section 2 of the Constitution, with respect to claiming someone relative to their service or labor, is closely mimicked in the Missouri Compromise.

By the 1830s, abolitionist activities continued to gain some momentum. In fact, from 1837 - 1838 some 130,000 petitions were sent to Congress on the subject of abolishing slavery in Washington, D.C. John C. Calhoun, a well-known politician and senator from South Carolina, rejected the sentiments of the many people who were calling for the abolition of slavery in the nation's capital. On March 9, 1836, in response to a petition from the Society of Friends, Calhoun argued that the Senate should not even receive the petition…

> "…why should these petitions be received? Why receive, when we have made up our mind not to act?"

---

[22] OurDocuments.gov. "Transcript of Missouri Compromise (1820)." Accessed May 2016.

Calhoun gave an impassioned speech which summed up his feelings of bigotry in a way that can only be shown via his own words.

> "If it should be such as I fear it will, if we receive this petition, and establish the principle that we are obliged to receive all such petitions, if we shall determine to take permanent jurisdiction over the subject of abolition, whenever and in whatever manner the abolitionists may ask, either here or in the States, I fear that the consequence will be ultimately disastrous. Such a course would destroy the confidence of the people of the slaveholding States in this Government. We love and cherish the Union; we remember with the kindest feelings our common origin, with pride our common achievements, and fondly anticipate the common greatness and glory that seem to await us; but origin, achievements, and anticipation of coming greatness, are to us as nothing, compared to this question. It

is to us a vital question. It involves not only our liberty, but, what is greater, (if to freemen any thing can be,) **existence itself. The relation which now exists between the two races in the slaveholding States has existed for two centuries. It has grown with our growth and strengthened with our strength. It has entered into and modified all our institutions, civil and political. None other can be substituted. We will not, cannot, permit it to be destroyed.** If we were base enough to do so, we would be traitors to our section, to ourselves, our families, and to posterity. It is our anxious desire to protect and preserve this relation by the joint action of the Government and the confederated States of the Union; but if instead of closing the door, if instead of denying all jurisdiction and all interference in this question, the doors of Congress are to be thrown open, and if we are to be exposed here, in the heart of the Union, to an endless attack on our rights, our character, and our institutions; if the other States are to stand and look on, without attempting to suppress these attacks, originating within their borders; and, finally, if this is to be our fixed and permanent condition, as members of this confederacy, we will the be compelled to turn our eyes on ourselves. Come what will, should it cost every drop of blood, and every cent of property, we must defend ourselves; and, if compelled, we would stand justified by all laws, human and divine."[23]

Here was a congressman equating slavery in the slaveholding states with "existence itself" and vowing that the relationship that existed in those states would be defended with "every drop of blood and every cent of property."

---

[23] A Century of Lawmaking for a New Nation: U.S. Congressional Documents and Debates, 1774 - 1875. Register of Debates, Senate, 24th Congress, 1st Session. Pages 765, 766, & 777. https://memory.loc.gov/cgi-bin/ampage?collId=llrd&fileName=022/llrd022.db&recNum=386

Calhoun was no "fly-by-night" politician—he was a member of the U.S. House of Representatives, Secretary of War, twice Vice President of the United States, Secretary of State under President John Tyler and a U. S. Senator during his life. He was also one of the most outspoken supporters of slavery throughout his political career.

John Calhoun believed that even accepting abolitionist petitions was a danger, in his words, "to the Union itself."

The result of all of these discussions in the House and in the Senate was that by May of 1836, the House of Representatives implemented a **"gag rule,"** which meant that no "resolutions regarding slavery" would be acted upon or even discussed for the next eight years, until December of 1844 when John Quincy Adams gathered enough votes to overturn the rule.

In 1850, the country again found itself having to deal with the issue of expansion and again, Henry Clay, called the "Great Compromiser," offered resolutions. The resolutions that Clay proposed were defeated as a package, but Senator Stephen Douglass, from Illinois, came forward with separate bills that were able to be enacted into law. So, the Compromise of 1850 resulted in:

- California being admitted as a free state and a territorial government being established in Utah;
- the settling of a boundary dispute between Texas and New Mexico and the establishment of a territorial government in New Mexico;
- and the suppression (not the elimination) of the slave trade in Washington, D.C. and amendments to the 1793 Fugitive Slave Act.

California was admitted into the Union in 1850.

The compromise also upheld the concept of popular sovereignty, which meant that voters could decide whether they wanted slavery within their borders. This, therefore, gave white males the ability to determine if other men and women would be enslaved in these new areas.

The action, however, that sent the most dramatic shock waves through the hearts and minds of black Americans was the way in which the Fugitive Slave Act was amended.

As we have mentioned, it was generally accepted that the Constitution called for the return of anyone who was in slavery (bound to service or labor by the laws of any state), who would escape to another state for their freedom. In 1793, George Washington signed the Fugitive Slave Act which helped to put more structure around the capture of enslaved people who escaped, but southern states were not satisfied given the growing amount of resistance throughout the country.

Thus, the Fugitive Slave Act of 1850:

- required U.S. authorities and commissioners to participate in the return of anybody, assumed to be a slave, to the person, legally, claiming such person as their slave;

- required marshals and deputy marshals to comply with the law and, if they refused, they could face a possible $1,000 fine;

- it authorized authorities to summon "bystanders" or citizens to help execute this law, "...all good citizens are hereby commanded to aid and assist in the prompt and efficient execution of this law, whenever their services are required...";

- it provided for trials and hearings to be held to determine the outcome of each case, but ordered that the person who had been captured could not testify on their own behalf; "In no trial or hearing under this act shall the testimony

> of such alleged fugitive be admitted in evidence;..."

This meant that any black person, on the streets of any city in America, could be captured, claimed as someone's property, and not be allowed to testify on their own behalf during the trial or hearing. This made many black people, Harriet Tubman included, seek shelter in Canada.

Furthermore, in 1854 the Kansas-Nebraska Act was passed. This act stipulated that the territories of Nebraska and Kansas, which were above the 36 degree, 30 minute line noted in the Missouri Compromise, *could* have slavery in their borders if the majority of voters decided to do so.[24]

> "it being the true intent and meaning of this act not to legislate slavery into any Territory or State, nor to exclude it therefrom, but to leave the people thereof perfectly free to form and regulate their domestic institutions in their own way, subject only to the

---

[24] Ourdocuments.gov National Archives and Records Administration. Kansas-Nebraska Act. Accessed May 2016.

Constitution of the United States:"[25]

Leaving "the people thereof perfectly free" to vote, meant that white males (over the age of twenty-one) would decide on the fate of others.

For a black person, who was fighting against slavery, this was a clear indication that the political leaders of the country were not going to side with your rights or your voice in this matter, as the law stipulated that only free white males (who met certain qualifications) could vote in the first elections which would determine whether or not slavery would exist in these territories.

This also infuriated anti-slavery activists, and northerners, who did not wish to see the spread of slavery and those who did not wish to compete with slave labor in new territories.

This led to the infiltration of Kansas, in particular, by both pro-slavery and anti-slavery forces—which resulted in bloody clashes and the eventual rise of the Republican Party.

The clashes were not confined to the streets. In May of 1856, Senator Charles Sumner gave an

---

[25] Ibid.

anti-slavery speech called, "The Crime Against Kanas," in which he mockingly accused Senators Stephen Douglas, of Illinois, and Andrew Butler, of South Carolina, of championing human wrongs by supporting the expansion of slavery.[26]

Two days later, on May 22, 1856, Representative Preston Brooks came into the Senate Chamber and beat Charles Sumner, savagely, over the head with a cane. Sumner barely saw him coming and was unable to defend himself against the attack. Sumner was badly injured and took years to recover, while Brooks (a relative of Andrew Butler) eventually resigned from his position in the House of Representatives, but was reelected to fill the vacancy caused by his own resignation.[27]

If all of this wasn't enough, the Supreme Court weighed in on the issue of slavery and territorial disputes around whether or not slavery could be prohibited in a given territory or newly

---

[26] Sumner, Charles. *The Crime Against Kansas: Speech of Hon. Charles Sumner in the Senate of the United States, 19th and 20th May, 1856.* Boston: John P. Jewett and Co., 1856.

[27] United States Senate. Senate History. "1851 - 1877: May 22, 1856, The Caning of Senator Charles Sumner." Accessed May 2016. http://www.senate.gov/artandhistory/history/minute/The_Caning_of_Senator_Charles_Sumner.htm

admitted state, in the famous Dred Scott case. Dred Scott was owned by a man who was a surgeon in the U.S. Army named Dr. Emerson. In 1834, Emerson took Scott from Missouri, where slavery was legal, to Illinois. Then, in 1836, Dr. Emerson took Dred Scott to Fort Snelling, a military post in what is today Minnesota. This territory was above the 36 degree, 30 minute line established as a part of the earlier Missouri Compromise. Also, in 1836, Dr. Emerson bought a woman named Harriet, who was also being held as a slave at Fort Snelling by someone else.

Dred Scott and Harriet got married in 1836 and in 1838 they had their first child, Eliza. That same year Dr. Emerson took them back to the state of Missouri, where they had their second daughter, Lizzie (Lizzie and Eliza were seven years apart). Dred Scott and his wife, Harriet, sued for their freedom and the freedom of their daughters. They argued that since they were held in slavery in areas where slavery was outlawed and then returned to a slave state, that their enslavement was illegal. In a case that took years to resolve, the Supreme Court handed down a decision on March 6, 1857.

The Supreme Court ruled:

- "A free negro of the African race, whose ancestors were brought to this country and sold as slaves, is not a 'citizen' within the meaning of the Constitution of the United States."

- "When the Constitution was adopted, they were not regarded in any of the States as members of the community which constituted the State, and were not numbered among its 'people or citizen.' Consequently, the special rights and immunities guaranteed to citizens do not apply to them. And not being 'citizens' within the meaning of the Constitution, they are not entitled to sue in that character in a court of the United States, and the Circuit Court has not jurisdiction in such a suit."

- "The only two clauses in the Constitution which point to this race, treat them as persons whom it was morally lawful to deal in as articles of property and to hold as slaves."

- "The plaintiff having admitted, by his demurrer to the plea in abatement, that his ancestors were imported from Africa and sold as slaves, he is not a citizen of the State of Missouri according to the Constitution of the United States, and was not entitled to sue in that character in the Circuit Court."

- "The act of Congress, therefore, prohibiting a citizen of the United States from taking with him his slaves when he removes to the Territory in question to reside, is an exercise of authority over private property which is not warranted by the Constitution-- and the removal of the plaintiff, by his owner, to that Territory, gave him no title to freedom."[28]

---

[28] Library of Congress. Primary Documents in American History. "Dred Scott v. John F. A. Sanford."

Thus, the Supreme Court, in 1857, ruled that even free African Americans were not citizens of the United States and that the Missouri Compromise which prohibited slavery in certain areas of the country was unconstitutional. Thus, Harriet Tubman had in front of her a monumental task—she was facing a government that was clearly not in support of her rights as a human being and she was living in a society that saw her as not equal. She would go on to do remarkable things with her life, despite facing incredible racism and discrimination.

Chapter 4:

The Place Where Harriet Tubman Was Born

Ironically, Harriet Tubman was born some 40 miles south of where Frederick Douglass was born, along the eastern shore of the Chesapeake Bay in Maryland. Douglass was born about four or five years before Tubman, but he gives a poignant description in his autobiography of what it was like to grow up in this area. He spoke of what it was like to not have a father figure in his life and to be forced into ignorance—even when it comes to knowing your own birthday.

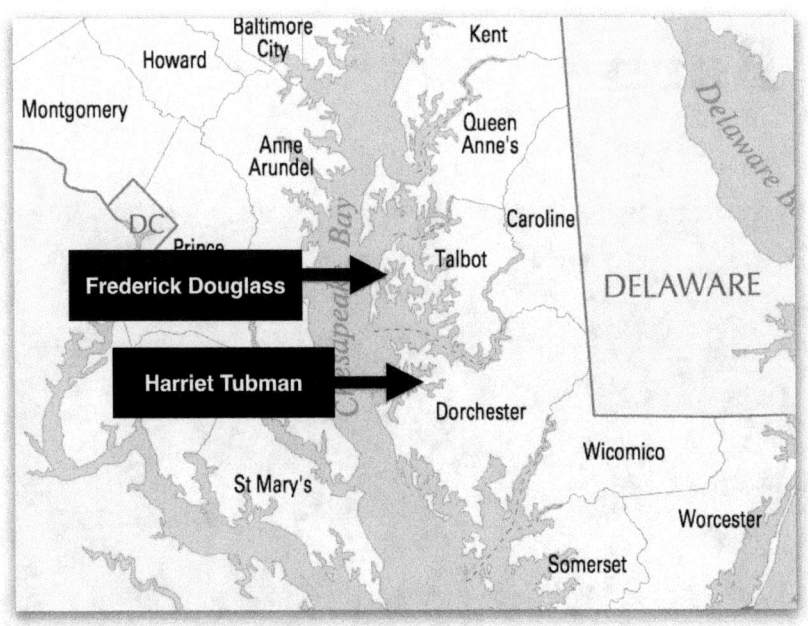

Douglass was born in Talbot County, Maryland and Harriet Tubman was born in Dorchester County.

"A person of some consequence here in the north, sometimes designated *father*, is literally abolished in slave law and slave practice. It is only once in a while that an exception is found to this statement. I never met with a slave who could tell me how old he was. Few slave-mothers know anything of the months of the year, nor of the days of the month. They keep no family records, with marriages, births, and deaths. They measure the ages of their children by spring time, winter time, harvest time, planting time, and the like; but these soon become undistinguishable and forgotten. Like other slaves, I cannot tell how old I am. This destitution was among my earliest troubles. I learned when I grew up, that my master—and this is the case with masters generally—allowed no questions to be put to him, by which a slave might learn his age. Such questions deemed evidence of impatience, and even of impudent curiosity. From certain events, however, the dates of which I have since learned, I suppose myself to have been born about the year 1817."[29]

---

[29] Douglass, Frederick. *My Bondage and My Freedom*. 1855.

Talbot County, MD where Frederick Douglass was born.

Harriet Tubman was no exception, she too never knew exactly when she was born, but her situation was extraordinary in that she had a lifelong relationship with her mother and father.

Harriet Tubman's parents were both born, most likely, in the 1780s—just as the United States was becoming a new country.

Harriet's father, Ben Ross, was enslaved by a man named Anthony Thompson, who was a member of the timber industry in Dorchester County. Thompson's business harvested timber for shipyards in Baltimore (and other businesses) and Ben Ross was one of his most valuable slaves.

Ross oversaw a good deal of the cutting, hauling, and transportation of Thompson's timber and was seen as a highly skilled worker.[30]

Some businessmen in the area turned to different sources of income, as tobacco had exhausted the soil.

Harriet's mother, Rit Green ("Rit" was short for Harriet), was originally enslaved by Atthow Pattison, but when he died he left her, and any

---

[30] Larson, Kate Clifford. *Bound for the Promise Land.* New York: Ballantine Books, 2004.

children she would have, to his granddaughter, Mary Pattison. Atthow also put a provision in his will that called for the manumission of Rit and her children, when they reached the age of forty-five, **but that provision was never honored.**

Mary Pattison married a man whose last name was Brodess and the two of them had a son named Edward Brodess. Mary's first husband died and she later went on to marry Anthony Thomspon—which is how Ben Ross and Harriet "Rit" Green met.

Mary Pattison did not live for very long after she married Anthony Thompson and he, thus, was left with the responsibility of caring for her son, Edward Brodess, and his inheritance (which included Harriet Green and any children she would have).

Edward Brodess was still a young boy when his mother died and he could, therefore, not take charge of his inheritance until he was older. This gave Harriet Green and Ben Ross some stability as a family, but that stability would eventually be challenged.

Ben and Rit, throughout their lives, would go on to have nine children:

- Linah (in approx. 1808)
- Mariah (in approx. 1811)
- Soph (in approx. 1813)
- Robert (in approx. 1815)
- Harriet, who was born Araminta and was affectionately called, "Minty," by her family. She would take on the name, Harriet Tubman, later on in life (was born most likely in 1822)
- Ben (in approx. 1823)
- Rachel (in approx. 1825)
- Henry (in approx. 1829 or 30)
- Moses (in approx. 1832)[31]

---

[31] Ibid.

Once Edward Brodess became old enough, he moved to a property, not far from Thompson's home, in another part of the county. Rit and her children, including Harriet ("Minty"), went to Brodess' farm.

Rit and her children lived here, for sometime, during the early part of Harriet's life.

Brodess often hired out the enslaved men and women he owned to do work for other people, as his farm was not very big and he needed the money. Harriet was subjected to this practice at a very young age.

Her Childhood

At the age of six, Brodess sent her to a man, who lived near by, to learn the craft of weaving from the man's wife. In many situations enslaved people did much of the weaving of the cloths that were needed in the homes of their owners. So, Harriet was going to be trained in this craft. When Harriet got there, the man also wanted her to take care of his muskrat traps, that were placed out in the marshes.

Marshes along the Eastern Shore.

Harriet was only six, but he sent her into the marshes, despite the weather conditions, to watch and manage his traps. She became ill and came down with a case of the measles. Harriet's mother found out about her daughter's condition and convinced Brodess to let Harriet come back to his farm, which he did. When Harriet got well, she was sent back, again, to the man's home.

When Harriet's first job (or contract) was finished, she was again sent to a stranger's home. At this new place, she was responsible for caring for a baby. Harriet was still a child herself and had to sit on the floor, to hold the baby, because she was not big enough to hold the child properly.

One day, while waiting for instructions from the child's mother, Harriet stood in the kitchen as the woman argued with her husband. This woman was especially mean to Harriet, so Harriet did not dare to interrupt her during their argument—she just waited. While standing there, she noticed a bowl on the table, filled with sugar. Harriet had never tasted sugar before, in her life, and her childhood curiosity got the best of her. She took a piece of sugar to see what it would taste like. As she grabbed the sugar and began to put it in her mouth, the woman turned around and saw Harriet.

Harriet knew what that meant. She ran out of the kitchen door and the woman and her husband chased her. Harriet did not stop because she knew they would beat her. She passed by homes where she could've stopped to take a rest, but she knew that they would send her back to the woman's home, so she kept running.

She ran, and ran, until she finally came to a pig pen on someone's property where she was just too tired to keep on going. She wasn't big enough to get over the fence, easily, but she made it up to the top and just fell over into the pen. She stayed there for two days, fighting the pigs for food, until she grew too hungry and decided to return. Once she got back, the woman's husband beat her, violently.

Thus, Harriet had a series of challenging experiences as a child. She was beaten by strangers, forced to work under difficult conditions, and separated from her mother and her siblings, for long periods of time.

She had such a strong desire to see her family, once, that she snuck away when she was about eleven years old—even after being told she could not go to see them. It was November of 1833 and Harriet's mom, one of Harriet's sisters and her younger brothers were hired out to a neighboring farm.

Harriet wanted to visit them, so she snuck away. The night was November 12, 1833 and the Leonid meteor shower lit up the sky over parts of the United States. Harriet and her brothers were so afraid...they thought the world was coming to an end because she decided to sneak away and had defied orders.[32]

Harriet had to grow up quickly. She had to figure out ways, like many slaves, to survive under extremely challenging circumstances—situations that no child should have to face.

---

[32] Harriet Tubman Underground Byway. "Finding a Way to Freedom: Driving Tour." http://harriettubmanbyway.org.

An area near the location of Harriet Tubman's childhood.

On another occasion, a woman came to Brodess' farm looking for someone to care for her child. She did not want to pay very much, so Brodess decided to send Harriet to work for the woman for a specific period of time.

Once Harriet arrived, it was clear that the lady wanted her to do more than just take care of her baby. Harriet was charged with doing the work around the house, as well. She was told to dust and sweep the parlor, as a part of her forced labor. She had never done this kind of housework before, so this was something new for her. After she swept the parlor, she began dusting right away; thinking this was the correct thing to do, however, when the woman came into the room, she noticed the furniture and room were still dusty and she was infuriated. She beat Harriet and made her do the dusting and the sweeping all over again. The same thing happened and, again, the woman beat her. The lady's sister happened to be visiting and she heard Harriet screaming in pain, so she stepped into the room to see what was going on. She asked her sister to leave the room. Then she asked Harriet how she was going about cleaning the parlor.

She told Harriet to first open the windows, then sweep. After sweeping she told her to go set the table in the other room, then return to the parlor to do the dusting...this way, the dust would have time to settle and the area could be wiped clean. She then explained to her sister that a little instruction and patience would have been better than simply beating Harriet.

At night, Harriet had to take care of the woman's baby as well. Harriet sat with the baby in her arms and would rock it to sleep. If the child woke up in the night and cried, the woman would beat Harriet with a whip that she kept close to her bed. She struck her mostly around her head and neck and Harriet bore some of those scars for the rest of her life.

The Blow to Her Head

Harriet was later sent to work on a farm, again, not far away from Brodess' home. Her job was to do farming work and she spent her time working in the fields. One evening, the plantation's cook came up to her and asked if she would go on a trip to the local store to pick up goods for the plantation. Harriet never really got a chance to take care of her hair; so she got a scarf, wrapped it around her head and went off to the store.

The store was located at a local intersection and, as soon as they arrived, they noticed a big commotion. An overseer, from another plantation, was chasing a slave who had left his farm without permission. The escaped slave had run into the store and the overseer was in hot pursuit. As Harriet walked inside the store, the overseer asked her to help him grab the man, but she refused. The man ran out of the door and, at that moment, the overseer picked up a heavy object on the countertop (probably a weight used to measure dry goods) and flung it at the man. Instead of hitting the man, it hit Harriet right in the head. She immediately fell to the ground and was unconscious. When she came to, she had blood all over her—the weight had cracked her skull, cut off a piece of the scarf she was wearing, and drove it right into her head.

The people around her picked her up and took her back to the plantation where she was working. She did not get any medical treatment, she was simply placed on a bench and left to rest.

She stayed on that bench the rest of the day and the entire next day, receiving no other kind of care. After two days, she was required to go back to work in the fields, although she was still bleeding and not fully recovered. Harriet was only about thirteen years old, at this time, and it was after this event that she began to have more vivid dreams and to hear the voice of God more clearly in her life.

Many people will say that she had dreams and visions that were largely attributable to this event and that the guidance given to her in those dreams was mainly coincidental, but I say that if her spiritual guidance allowed her to avoid capture so many times, then it was Providence, not coincidence, that guided her throughout her life.

After the blow to the head, she also began to have long periods of time where she would "blackout" and simply fall asleep. This made some people underestimate her intelligence and her abilities.

Adulthood

As she got older, she continued to be hired out to other places to work. She began to work with timber…cutting it down, stacking it, and hauling it. This brought her, again, closer to her father, who was still a well-respected timber worker. By 1840, Ben Ross was a free man; he was freed in the will of Anthony Thompson.

While working with timber Harriet met John Tubman. John was a free man, who was working as a timber laborer, when Harriet married him in 1844. It was at this time that she assumed the name Harriet instead of her birth name, Araminta. Harriet was her mom's name. She also took on Tubman's last name and therefore became known as Harriet Tubman.

As an enslaved person, Harriet was always at the mercy of someone else and when she became seriously ill, she was sent back to the Brodess farm. Edward Brodess decided that she was better off sold, than kept, and he began to entertain people who might consider buying Harriet—Brodess was also in a lot of debt.

Harriet was sick for months and was confined to a bed. While she laid there in bed, Brodess sent in potential buyers, every so often, to check her out to see if she was worth purchasing. Harriet was furious, and being a spiritual person and severely sick, she could only pray…there was nothing else she could do.

> "…as I lay sick on my bed, from Christmas till March, I was always praying for (Edward Brodess). 'Pears

like I didn't do nothing but pray for (him). Oh, Lord, convert (him); Oh, dear, Lord, change that man's heart, and make him a Christian. And all the time he was bringing men to look at me, and they stood there saying what they would give and what they would take, and all I could say was, 'Oh, Lord, convert (him).' Then I heard that as soon as I was able to move I was to be sent with my brothers, in the chain-gang to the far South. Then I changed my prayer, and I said, 'Lord, if you ain't never going to change that man's heart, kill him. Lord, and take him out of the way, so he won't do no more mischief.' Next thing I heard (he) was dead; and he died just as he had lived, a wicked, bad man."[33]

(Parentheses are mine).

So, Edward Brodess was dead and things were now very uncertain for Harriet and her family.

---

[33] Bradford, Sarah. *Harriet Tubman: The Moses of Her People.* 1886.

Sometime before he died, Harriet had an opportunity to save up money from the extra work she was able to do cutting and hauling wood. She hired a lawyer to look into her mother's past; she wanted to get an idea of how old her mother actually was. The lawyer looked back sixty years and couldn't find anything. She asked him to look back further and he did. He found Atthow Pattison's old will, where he gave Rit and her unborn children to his granddaughter, Mary. Harriet discovered the clause in Atthow's will that emancipated Rit and any children she would have, once they turned forty-five. She then believed that her mother and her family were being kept in slavery, illegally.

This may have been why Harriet felt, so strongly, that Brodess was an evil man; not to mention **the fact that he also sold, earlier, her older sisters—Linah, Mariah and Soph.**

Brodess was in debt and, after his death, his estate had to deal with the money he owed, which put a lot of pressure on his widow, Eliza Brodess.

The year was 1849 and Harriet believed that the death of Brodess meant that she and some members of her family were in real danger of being sold. She also felt more of a connection with God and perhaps felt some guilt for praying for Brodess' death. After she recovered from her illness, she began to pray continuously.

> "When I took up the towel to wipe my face and hands, I cried, 'Oh, Lord, for Jesus' sake, wipe away all my sins!' When I took up the broom and began to sweep, I groaned, 'Oh, Lord, whatsoever sin there be in my heart, sweep it out, Lord, clear and clean'; ..."[34]

Despite feeling closer to God, the fact still remained that she felt unsafe and believed that her and her brothers would be soon sold to slave traders (remember the demand in the South for enslaved workers to grow cotton was high). Harriet began to have dreams—in her dreams men and horses were chasing after her and there was an imaginary line separating the land of slavery, from the land of freedom. There were also kind and friendly Caucasian ladies on the other side, reaching out their hands to help her.

---

[34] Ibid.

The dreams and visions Harriet had fed her faith. She committed herself to trusting in the Lord, which was the basis of her courage.

> "I had reasoned this out in my mind; there was one of two things I had a right to, liberty, or death; if I could not have one, I would have the other; for no man should take me alive; I should fight for my liberty as long as my strength lasted, and when the time came for me to go, the Lord would let them take me."[35]

"They Should Be Free Also"

Harriet convinced her brothers, Henry and Ben, to leave with her. They started out hoping that people who sympathized with their cause would help them, but the journey was difficult and unfamiliar. After they left, Eliza Brodess, Edward's widow, placed an ad in the paper for their return. It read:

---

[35] Ibid.

THREE HUNDRED DOLLARS REWARD

"Ranaway from the subscriber on Monday the 17th ult., three negroes, named as follows: HARRY, aged 19 years, has on one side of his neck a wen, just under the ear, he is of a dark chestnut color, about 5 feet 8 or 9 inches height; BEN, aged about 25 years, is very quick to speak when spoken to, he is of chestnut color, about six feet high; MINTY, aged about 27 years, is of a chestnut color, fine looking, and about 5 feet high. One hundred dollars reward will be given for each of the above named negroes, if taken out of the State, and $50 each if taken in the State. They must be lodged in Baltimore, Easton or Cambridge Jail, in Maryland."

ELIZA ANN BRODESS,

Near Bucktown, Dorchester county, Md.

Oct. 3d, 1849

Yes, Harriet was about five feet tall.

Her brothers, Harry (Henry) and Ben, were afraid they would eventually get caught and convinced her to go back. However, shortly after returning with her brothers, she decided to go, again…this time alone.

By this time Ben, Harriet's father, was working for Anthony Thompson's son; still in the timber business, but now in the Poplar Neck area of Caroline County….a little farther north. Harriet may have been hired out in this area, as well, when she made her escape.

When she decided to go, she believed God would take care of her. She confided in a white local woman, whom she felt would be sympathetic to her cause.[36]

The woman, who may have been a Quaker, gave Harriet the names of two people who would help her and told her how to get to the first house…the people there would direct her to the second location.[37]

---

[36] Larson, Kate Clifford. *Bound for the Promise Land.* (New York: Ballantine Books, 2004), Chapter 4.

[37] Helen Tatlock, a neighbor of Harriet Tubman, later in life, granted an interview to E Conrad in which she revealed stories Harriet told her of that first successful escape.

Harriet wanted to tell some members of her family about her impending plans to leave, but she knew she could not tell her mother, because her mother would cry and alarm others for fear of losing her daughter. So, Harriet went to tell another family member, Mary, about her plans to leave. Mary worked in the kitchen on this plantation and when Harriet arrived, there were other people in the room…so she pretended to joke around and play with Mary and got Mary to go outside with her, but the owner rode up, just then, and she was unable to tell Mary outright. So, Harriet tried to tell her in a song…

"I'll meet you in the mornin'

When you reach the promised land;

On the other side of Jordan,

For I'm bound for the promised land."

Harriet was able to leave without that owner figuring out what she was about to do. She made her way to the first house. The woman there, fearing detection, told Harriet to sweep the yard…so her being there wouldn't seem strange.

When the woman's husband returned from work, he told Harriet to hide in his wagon under a cover, then he loaded up his wagon and took her to the next house.

This entire area was also home to many free blacks, who were closely tied to the enslaved men and women, and to Quakers who had denounced slavery. So Harriet may have had people scattered along the way, black and white, who were willing to risk their lives to help an escaping slave.

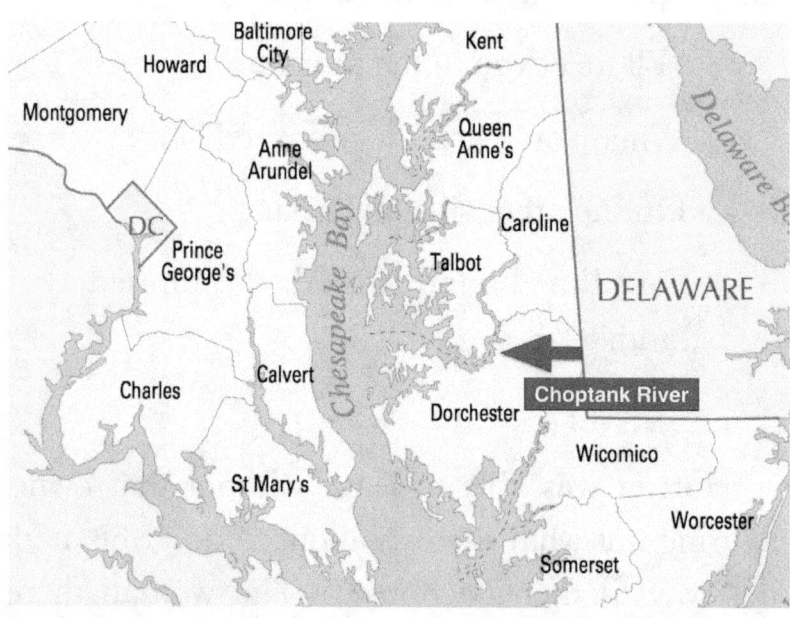

The Choptank River was a natural pathway that could be used as a guide north.

When she finally reached free territory, Harriet realized the awesomeness of being free and what she had accomplished. In her dreams the kind white ladies who would help her were now a reality and she was actually free and safe in northern territory.

She came to a conclusion that would then characterize the rest of her life.

> "I looked at my hands to see if I was the same person now I was free. There was such a glory over everything, the sun came like gold through the trees, and over the fields, and I felt like I was in heaven.
>
> (Thinking about her family)
>
> But to this solemn resolution I came, I was free and they should be free also."[38]

---

[38] Bradford, Sarah. *Harriet Tubman: The Moses of Her People.* 1886.

Near the area where Harriet Tubman was born and raised.

Chapter 5:

Solemn Resolution

Rochester, August 29, 1868

Dear Harriet:

"I am glad to know that the story of your eventful life has been written by a kind lady, and that the same is so soon to be published. You ask for what you do not need when you call upon me for a word of commendation. I need such words from you far more than you can need them from me, especially where your superior labors and devotion to the cause of the lately enslaved of our land are known as I know them. The difference between us is very marked. Most that I have done and suffered in the service of our cause has been public, and I have received much encouragement at every step of the way. You on the other hand have labored in a private way. I have wrought in the day--you in the night. I have had the applause of the crowd and the satisfaction that comes of being approved by the multitude, while the most that you have done has been witnessed by a few trembling, scarred, and foot-sore bondmen and women, whom you have led out of the house of bondage, and whose heartfelt 'God bless you' has been your only reward. The midnight sky and the silent stars have been the witnesses of your devotion to freedom and of your heroism. Excepting

John Brown--of sacred memory--I know of no one who has willingly encountered more perils and hardships to serve our enslaved people than you have. Much that you have done would seem improbable to those who do not know you as I know you. It is to me a great pleasure and a great privilege to bear testimony to your character and your works, and to say to those to whom you may come, that I regard you in every way truthful and trustworthy."

Your friend,

Frederick Douglass[39]

What Was it Like For Her to Rescue People From Maryland?

When a person decided to escape from slavery they were making a brave and harrowing decision. There was no way to know exactly how long it would take or whether the people you might meet would betray you. The only things you did know were that it was illegal to leave and that men

---

[39] Braford, Sarah. *Scenes in the Life of Harriet Tubman.* Auburn: W. J. Moses, Printer, 1869.

would most likely chase after you with all the fire power and resources they had at their disposal.

On the Eastern Shore the terrain was very challenging—it was filled with wetlands, waterways and wooded areas that could be both dangerous and useful.

Talbot County, Maryland.

Many times, if a person left, they did not have an opportunity to bring supplies such as food, clothes, water, shoes, or weapons for defense.

This is what Harriet Tubman was faced with when she would return to her home for rescues—many people came with simply the clothes on their backs and nothing else...some even came with small children.

Something as simple as walking around could be difficult given the areas where they had to hide.

Talbot County, Maryland, forest floor.

In addition, travelers had to make sure they were going in the right direction in order to go north. Their motivation, quick thinking and knowledge of the area helped them. Green growth can clearly be seen on one side of many trees in this area, which was an indication of which way the sun was shining—as the green growth would survive on the northern side of the trees, opposite the angle of the sun.

Also, the natural flow of the rivers helped to guide escapees north.

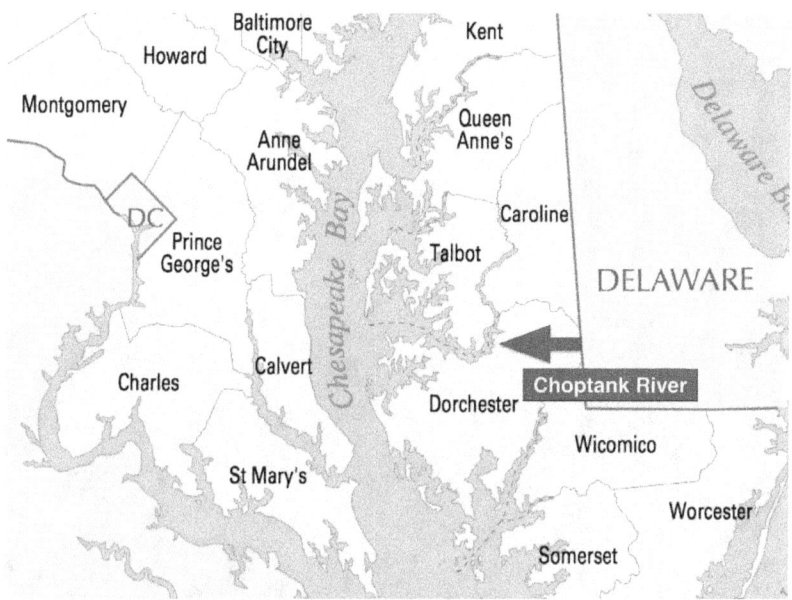

Harriet's father lived along the shores of the Choptank River and Harriet often used this river to guide her north. (See the banks of the Choptank River below).

Of course, many times escapees had to travel at night and the North Star helped to reaffirm the direction they needed to follow.

Grass along the Choptank River.

Snow-covered ground, Eastern Shore.

Harriet Tubman often travelled at night and many times, she would come to get her parties during the fall or winter months when the days were shorter and the nights longer—thus giving them more time to travel at night.

Bobcats, raccoons…animals that live in the water like muskrats, insect bites, etc. were all things you had to contend with if you traveled through the areas around the eastern shore of the Chesapeake Bay. Frostbite, hypothermia, and simply finding ways to get food were all things you had to address in addition to thinking about the men who were chasing you who would likely hurt you and bring you back into slavery, if they caught you.

Harriet carried a weapon with her; not just for the slave catchers who might find them, but for those who traveled with her because she said that dead people couldn't tell secrets. On one occasion she was due to meet a group in the woods, but for some reason they didn't show up. That night a terrible snow storm hit and Harriet was left in the woods, as she had been waiting for them. She asked "Jesus to take care of her" and took shelter beside a tree for the entire night. She said that her faith and her trust in God helped her to spend the entire night in the storm without getting frostbitten.

On a different occasion, she was leading a group of people when she got a bad feeling. She told them that they had to stop and cross the body of water that was in front of them. The steam was wide and appeared to be deep, with rapidly flowing waters. The men were afraid to cross, as they might get swept away, but they followed Harriet, since she went right into the waters. She recalled that as they all thought they were going to go under, the waters got shallower and shallower and the waters never, at any point, came above her chin.

She had to pass through another stream in the same manner and later she found out that advertisements had been placed for them in the direction that they were going and officers were waiting for them. The decision to cross the streams helped them avoid capture.

This gives you some idea of the kinds of dangerous situations she faced as she voluntarily came back into slave territory to lead other people away to freedom.

Her First Trip

Harriet began her journeys back by first helping her niece and her two children escape.

About a year after Harriet Tubman escaped in 1849, she learned that her niece (along with her two children) would be sold by Eliza Brodess. In December of 1850, Harriet Tubman was able to coordinate with Kessiah's husband, John Bowley (who was a free carpenter). Kessiah had been up for sale before.

> "I will sell at public sale to the highest bidder for cash, at the Court house door, in the town of Cambridge, on MONDAY the 10th day of September next, a negro woman named Kizziah, aged about 25 years. She will be sold for life, and a good title will be given. Attendance given by,
>
> John Mills
>
> Agent for Elizabeth Brodess
>
> August 29, 1849."[40]

---

[40] National Underground Railroad, Network to Freedom. "Kessiah's Flight." Historical marker.

Kessiah was going to be sold originally, but the event was cancelled. Edward Brodess's family challenged Eliza Brodess in court, claiming that they had a financial right to Rit and any of her children (Kessiah was Rit's granddaughter).

This time, however, in December of 1850... the sale was going to take place.

Dorchester County, Maryland

John Bowley coordinated with Harriet, as Harriet went to Baltimore and awaited Kessiah's arrival. Harriet stayed with friends, mostly likely Tom Tubman who was her husband's brother in Baltimore. On the day of the auction John

Bowley headed down to the courthouse in Dorchester and participated in the auction for his children and his wife. He won the bidding.

While things were being finalized, the auctioneer went to go eat over his break. When he returned he found that the man who bid for Kessiah and her two children did not come forward and he later discovered that the children and Kessiah were gone. John, who was very familiar with the waterways of the Eastern Shore, navigated his family through the waters of the Chesapeake Bay to Baltimore, in the cold of December. In Baltimore, they met up with Harriet Tubman and she guided them to Philadelphia a few days later.

Several months later, she came back to Baltimore and met up with her brother, Moses, and a couple of others and again led them to freedom. She would now turn her attention to the Eastern Shore and go directly into the area where she was enslaved to rescue other family members and friends. One such trip illustrates the types of challenges she faced when traveling into this dangerous area.

November 1856

A man named Josiah "Joe" Bailey was enslaved in Maryland's Eastern Shore, not far from where Harriet Tubman was born. Joe had been hired out to William Hughlett for six years.

During that time Joe was such an exceptionally skilled worker that he managed Hughlett's day-to-day operations and Hughlett did not bother hiring an overseer because Joe did the work for him. William Hughlett decided that he wanted to buy Joe, so he approached Joe's owner.

Joe's owner did not give in easily; he first raised the price, then negotiated, before he agreed to let Joe go for one thousand dollars down, and another thousand dollars in the future.

William Hughlett finalized the deal and the next morning he went to the slave quarters, where Joe was, to tell him about the change in ownership. He approached Joe, while he was inside eating. Joe heard Hughlett's voice and came outside. Hughlett told Joe that he now belonged to him and he then said, "Now, Joe, strip, and take a licking."

Joe hesitated.

"Haven't I worked through sun and rain, early in the morning and late at night; haven't I saved you an overseer by doing his work?"

"No, Joe, I have no complaint to make of you. …you've always worked well. But you belong to me now;…and the first lesson my (niggers) have to learn is that I am master and they belong to me, and are never to resist anything I order them to do."

Joe knew what the consequences would be for disobeying his orders, so he took off his clothes and got a beating from William Hughlett.

Frustrated and still bleeding, Joe snuck into a canoe that night and rowed six miles to the area of Poplar Neck, where Ben Ross (Harriet's father) lived.

When he got there, he told Ben, "Next time (your daughter) 'Moses' comes, let me know."

Ben Ross apparently assisted him, and many others, in their escapes.[41]

Harriet did come some three weeks later and on November 15, 1856, Joe Bailey, his brother

---

[41] Maryland State Archives, MSA SC 5496-1535. Josiah "Joe" Bailey (b. 1828 - d. ?). "Fled from slavery, Talbot County, Maryland, 1856."

William Bailey, Peter Pennington, and Eliza Manokey all joined Harriet Tubman on a journey on the Underground Railroad.

The shores of the Choptank River.
This is near the likely location of Ben Ross' home, in Poplar Neck, Caroline County, MD.

As we have mentioned, the road to freedom from this area of Maryland was treacherous. It was no easy task and Harriet and her travelers would be tested, in almost every way, during their journey.

Slave catchers were in "hot pursuit" from almost the very beginning of their journey. They hid in natural hiding places during the day, while the catchers were within a few feet of them. At times they were forced to separate, taking orders from Harriet to go by foot or wagon or boat to specific locations.

At one point in the journey, Harriet began to experience an intense headache and collapsed in front of her group. They were frantic and some of them wanted to leave her and to keep moving, but Joe convinced them not to. She eventually woke up and continued right on the path she was following.

They reached Delaware, but came to a difficult spot at a bridge that crossed the Christiana River in Wilmington, DE. Harriet immediately told the group to hide because the bridge was being guarded by policemen...since it was an area where escaped slaves would frequently cross.

Harriet told Joe and the others to separate, and to go to different houses, until she gave them further instructions. She then sent a message to Thomas Garrett, a well-known abolitionist and supporter of the Underground Railroad...he was someone she worked closely with on various occasions. Garrett helped slaves as they crossed through Delaware, and years earlier, he was sued and convicted for aiding slaves.

Thomas Garrett gathered a group of African-American bricklayers, as well as Caucasian workers. Garrett owned a shop near the bridge and often gave escaped slaves shoes and other supplies to help them on their trips. He asked the bricklayers to pretend as if they were on a job.

The next day the bricklayers crossed the bridge, singing and talking loudly, as the police officers inspected their wagon. In the evening they came back across the bridge, this time carrying Harriet, Joe, and the others in the wagon...hidden underneath the straw. The police did not bother to inspect the wagon again, as the workers were still loud and singing....acting as if they were drunk. Once they reached Garrett, he gave them supplies and helped them on their way.

In the meantime, William Hughlett, and two others, put out an ad. It read:

TWO THOUSAND SIX HUNDRED DOLLARS REWARD

Ran away from the subscriber, on Saturday night. November 15th, 1856, JOSIAH and WILLIAM BAILEY, and PETER PENNINGTON. Joe is about 5 feet 10 inches in height, of a chestnut color, bald head, with a remarkable scar on one of his cheeks, not positive on which it is, but think it is on the left, under the eye; has intelligent countenance, active and we'll made. He is about 28 years old. Bill is of a darker color, about 5 feet 8 inches in height, stammers a little when confused, well made and older than Joe; well dressed, but may have pulled kearsey on over their other clothes. Peter is smaller than either the others, about 25 years of age, dark chestnut color, 5 feet 7 or 8 inches high.

A reward of fifteen hundred dollars will be given to any person who will apprehend the said Joe Bailey and lodge him safely in the jail at Easton, Ta'bot co., Md., and $300 for Bill and $800 for Peter.

W.R. Hughlett,

John C. Henry,

T. Wright.

Trappe, Talbot co., Md.. Nov. 18th, 1856. n22-9t*1

(William Hughlett, John Henry, and T. Wright placed an ad in the Baltimore Sun, on November 18, 1856, for the capture and return of Josiah, William and Peter.[42])

Harriet and her "passengers" made it to Philadelphia, where they met up with William Still. Still would also become well-known for his support of, and participation in, the Underground Railroad. He helped escaped slaves and kept records of the people he met and their stories.

---

[42] Maryland State Archives, MSA SC 5496-1535. Josiah "Joe" Bailey (b. 1828 - d. ?). "Fled from slavery, Talbot County, Maryland, 1856." Accessed September 2013.

He, at times, tried to keep the involvement of Harriet Tubman a secret, in his records, so as not to endanger her further. Joe and his brother sat down and told William Still their story,[43] and all that had transpired, but the time came for them to leave before he could document Eliza's and Peter's story. William Still gave Joe and his brother $3.25 and Harriet, $2.50.

The next location where they were able to get some help was at the local Anti-Slavery office in New York. Oliver Johnson, another active abolitionist, recognized Joe, as soon as he walked into the door. "Well, I am glad to see the man who is worth (so much) to his master." exclaimed Oliver. Joe was frightened. How could he be recognized this far away from Maryland? Oliver Johnson told him he had a copy of the ad in the office and it described him so well, that he knew he must be Joe Bailey.

Joe was concerned. It was 1856 and the Fugitive Slave Act of 1850 was in full effect. So, Joe wanted to know how far it was to Canada, since that was their final destination. They told him it was another 300 miles, by train, to get to

---

[43] Still, William. *The Underground Railroad: A Record of Facts, Authentic Narratives, Letters, etc.* (Philadelphia: Porter & Coates, 1872), pp. 272-274.

Canada and Joe couldn't believe it. They continued through the state of New York to Albany and then to Syracuse, finally making it to Niagara. Canada was under British rule at the time and the British royal coat of arms contained a lion, with a paw prominently displayed. Joe was worried the entire way through New York and, no matter how much the others tried to cheer him up, he was too concerned about being captured.

Once they got to the suspension bridge, separating New York from Canada, everyone else started to rejoice. They weren't officially in Canada until they passed the halfway point of the bridge, so Joe didn't celebrate.

Niagara Falls, New York.

At a certain spot on the bridge, everyone could see Niagara Falls. The others were so excited to see this natural wonder, but Joe didn't look. Harriet tried to get him to look, but he wouldn't turn his head!

Once they got far enough across the bridge, Harriet said to Joe, "Joe! You've shook the lion's paw! You're a free man!"

Joe realized he was in Canada and was ecstatic. The others began to celebrate and, once they got off of the bridge, everyone crowded around Harriet—thanking her for all her help. Joe was so excited...Harriet could only see Joe, singing and walking off into the distance, saying, "There is only one more journey for me now, and that's to heaven!"[44]

Harriet made the trip, from Canada to the Eastern Shore, at least eleven times and she made at least several more trips from other locations.

While she was in between trips, she often got work as domestic worker in a hotel or some other establishment, in Philadelphia or New Jersey, to gain extra money for her trips.

---

[44] Bradford, Sarah. *Harriet Tubman: The Moses of Her People.* 1886.

After helping to free her niece, Kessiah, in 1850, it is believed that Harriet:[45]

- helped to free her brother, Moses, and others in early 1851;
- escorted eleven people to freedom in late 1851;
- had as many as nine people in her fall of 1852 trip;
- made another trip in June of 1854:
- in December of 1854 helped to free her brothers, Robert, Henry and Benjamin, Jr. (and others);
- came back to free more in early 1855;
- in December of 1855, made another trip to free people;
- in May of 1856 may have had at least four people on this trip;
- in October of 1856 came back again;
- returned again in November of 1856 and rescued Joe Bailey, his brother William Bailey, Eliza Manokey and

---

[45] Larson, Kate Clifford. *Bound for the Promise Land.* New York: Ballantine Books, 2004.

Peter Pennington;

- in May of 1857 (she helped her father and mother leave the area because she believed her father was in impending danger);

- in November of 1860 she had perhaps seven on this trip including a man, his wife and their three children (a girl who was six, a child who was four and a three-month-old infant).[46]

---

[46] Still, William. *The Underground Railroad: A Record of Facts, Authentic Narratives, Letters, etc.* Philadelphia: Porter & Coates, 1872.

Chapter 6:

Harriet's Parents, Other Heroes and The Dover Eight

In addition to directly helping many men, women and children escape, Harriet Tubman also provided directions through her underground network that led to the successful escapes of dozens of other people.

Her network of supporters was effective, she received help from many people as she travelled up and down the Mid-Atlantic and Northeastern portions of the United States. When she arrived in the Eastern Shore, she often left from the area near where her father lived, in Poplar Neck, along the Choptank river (on a couple of occasions she left from Baltimore as we have mentioned).

While in the Eastern Shore during her journeys, if she was near enough, one of the homes she would stop at for assistance was the home of Samuel Green. Green was an African-American man who helped many men and women escape from the Eastern Shore.

She would then go to Sandtown, Delaware where she might meet Will Grove and then on to Camden, DE where Nat and William Brinkley (two brothers) would give her help. In Wilmington, DE she often received assistance from Thomas Garrett who was a Quaker and a dedicated anti-slavery supporter.

As she made her way through Delaware, she would then go to Philadelphia where she would meet with William Still and members of the Vigilance Committee. Still, as we mentioned, was an African-American man who documented the many men, women and children he helped as they came through Philadelphia. In 1872, he published a book about his experiences entitled, *The Underground Railroad*.

After leaving Philadelphia, Harriet might head toward New York, where she received help from many important anti-slavery activists there and then she would go through upstate New York where she received assistance from many people, including Frederick Douglass who was living in Rochester. From there, she would make her way across the border, to Canada, where communities of free blacks were established—especially after the passage of the Fugitive Slave Act of 1850.

Harriet Tubman met many men and women through her efforts—from Boston to Maryland… from Philadelphia to Canada. Her work had to largely be done in secret as she was never legally free in the United Staes until after the Emancipation Proclamation and the Civil War.

Samuel Green

Samuel Green was a well-respected man and a former slave, who had obtained his own freedom. He was also able to buy the freedom of his wife and he built up a respectable reputation, for himself, amongst the local population.

Green provided his home as a safe harbor for slaves trying to escape north, and on several occasions, he allowed Harriet Tubman to use his place as a safe house, when she came to rescue others from the area.

Sam and his wife, Catherine, had two children, Samuel Jr. and a daughter named, Susan. By 1842 both Sam and Catherine were free, but their children, Sam Jr. and Susan were still enslaved. On one of her journeys back to the Eastern Shore, Harriet gave Sam Jr., and his father, very specific information about how to get north without being captured and, in 1854, Sam Green Jr. decided to take her advice. He escaped, made his way to Philadelphia (were he also met and received help from William Still), and eventually made it all the way to Canada. Susan, however, was sold to someone in Missouri, after her brother's escape.

Samuel Green was a strong man and he did not let the fate of his daughter stop him from secretly working to help others escape. In an interesting twist, Samuel Green Jr. actually knew Josiah "Joe" Bailey and mentioned him in a letter to his father, after his escape.

In fact, Sam Sr. helped Harriet Tubman, Joe Bailey and the others in their escape, in 1856— two years after his son escaped.

These activities would prove to be costly for Samuel Green. In the winter of 1856 - 1857, Sam Green went to visit his son in Canada and upon his return the situation with the Dover Eight (whom we will discuss shortly) caused so much commotion that Sam was suspected of aiding and abetting in their escape. His home was searched by the sheriff based on the suspicion that he aided fugitive slaves. Letters from his son were found, a map, and at least one volume of *Uncle Tom's Cabin*.[47] Green was arrested on April 4, 1857 and was charged with crimes related to the possession of "a certain abolitionist pamphlet called Uncle Tom's Cabin...calculated to create discontent amongst the colored population."[48]

He was found guilty of one of his charges and later, on May 14, 1857, was sentenced to a minimum of ten years in prison in the Maryland Penitentiary. He may have been the only person, in U.S. history, to be convicted of simply possessing an anti-slavery piece of literature. There wasn't enough evidence to argue, in court, that he aided fugitive slaves, but his efforts were an example of the cunningness and intelligence used by he and others, like Harriet Tubman, to avoid detection and to help others gain their freedom. In 1862, Governor Augustus Bradford issued a pardon for Samuel Green on the condition that he leave the state of Maryland

---

[47] Maryland State Archives, MSA SC 3520-13785. Samuel Green (b. 1802 - d. 1877). "Arrested for possession of Uncle Tom's Cabin, Dorchester County, 1857, Alleged accomplice to slave flight, 1854 - 1857." http://msa.maryland.gov/megafile/msa/speccol/sc3500/sc3520/013700/013785/html/13785bio.html

[48] Ibid.

within sixty days. There are so many examples of heroism that grew out of the resistance to slavery, that many of us would be forever inspired if we knew about all of the men and women who resisted.

The Dover Eight

Henry Predeaux was enslaved in the Bucktown area in Dorchester County. This is the same area of Maryland where Harriet and her family were enslaved on Edward Brodess' farm. Henry's owner, one day, threatened to sell him south and in March of 1857 Henry decided to escape.[49] He was a large man, about 27 years old, and was determined to seek his freedom using the network of people who were willing to try to help escaped slaves. He was also able to get instructions from Harriet Tubman…probably through her father, and he likely received help from Samuel Green.

Henry Predeaux set out on his journey with Thomas Elliot, Denard Hughes, Lavina Woolfley, James Woolfley, Bill Kiah, Emily Kiah, and at least one other person.

These eight travelers made the long journey through the landscape of the Eastern Shore… navigating the wetlands, the wooded areas, and its marshes. When they arrived in Dover, Delaware they were instructed to meet up with a man by the name of Thomas Otwell. The eight men and

---

[49] Still, William. *The Underground Railroad: A Record of Facts, Authentic Narratives, Letters, etc.* Philadelphia: Porter & Coates, 1872.

women had been given instructions by Harriet Tubman, undoubtedly given to them through other people, and they followed the instructions every step of the way. When they arrived in Delaware, they did not necessarily suspect that there would be any undue trouble.

Thomas Otwell was a black man who knew Harriet Tubman and apparently helped her on several of her journeys through Delaware. Many times Harriet, Thomas Garrett, and others would pay people to perform certain tasks in support of the Underground Railroad—housing or picking up someone, escorting escapees to different places, etc. These tasks were rewarded with a little bit of money to help ensure the assignment got completed and to provide the person with some type of reward for the risks they were undertaking.

By the time the eight men and women reached Dover, there was a $3,000 reward for their arrest.[50] Thomas Otwell was supposed to meet the Dover Eight and take them to the home of William Brinkley (whom we've mentioned), an African-American man who sometimes helped

[50] Ibid.

escaped slaves get through that part of Delaware. Otwell, instead of taking the eight people to Brinkley's house, led them to the local jail.

He had notified the sheriff and others, ahead of time, that he would be bringing by the escapees. It was night time, and it was a little difficult to see, as Otwell led them up the stairs...remarking that they were "cold, but would soon have a good warming." Once they got in, a light was lit and the eight men and women noticed the iron bars.

A brutal fight broke out between the would-be captives and the sheriff and his men. The group managed to make it down one flight of stairs and the brawl continued into the sheriff's private apartment.

The sheriff's wife and children were awakened and they began screaming and were scared for their lives. Henry noticed a "shovel of fire" (used to help keep fire places going at that time) and spread its contents all over the floor. This gave them a little bit of time. The two women jumped through the window. Henry then picked up an andiron (heavy iron supports used to hold wood inside a fireplace) and smashed out the rest of the window, through which the other men jumped. The distance to the ground was about twelve feet and each of them made it out. Upon hitting the ground they were faced with a wall surrounding the jail, but desperate times will bring out the best of physical efforts. Seven of them made it over the wall…six of them managed to run off together but, for one of them, it was unclear where he went.

By the time Henry got on the other side of the wall, the sheriff was there facing him. The sheriff stood there, "…in his stockings without his shoes" and pointed his pistol at Henry, but the gun did not go off. Henry was able to get away.

Letter from Thomas Garrett

Wilmington, 3d mo. 13th, 1857 (March 1857)

Dear Cousin, Samuel Rhoads:

I have a letter this day from an agent of the Underground Rail Road, near Dover,…saying I must be on the look out for six brothers and two sisters, they were decoyed and betrayed, he says by a colored man named Thomas Otwell, who pretended to be their friend, and sent a white (man) ahead to wait for them at Dover till they arrived; they were arrested...

....they broke jail; six of them are secreted in the neighborhood, and the writer has not known what became of the other two. The six were to start last night for this place. I hear that their owners have persons stationed at several places on the road watching. I fear they will be taken.... I shall have two men sent this evening some four or five miles below to keep them away from this town,...

Thee may show this to Still (William Still) and McKim, and oblige thy cousin,

Thomas Garrett.

(parentheses are mine)

Here, again, Thomas Garrett played an important role in helping to keep runaway slaves safe from harm and further aided them on their pathway to freedom.

The majority of the Dover Eight (including Henry) made it to William Still and the Vigilance Committee in Philadelphia. William Still documented their story and sent them on their way with help from the committee. Several of the "Eight" were confirmed to have made it all the way to Canada, but nothing is known of what happened to Henry Predeaux after 1857.[51]

Many abolitionists used the story of the Dover Eight to help further their cause, but the slaveholders of the Eastern Shore were equally committed.[52]

Back in the Eastern Shore Samuel Green, as we have mentioned, was suspected of helping the Dover Eight escape. Harriet feared that her father might also be implicated.

---

[51] Maryland State Archives. MSA SC 5496-7978. Henry Predeaux (b. circa 1830 - d. ?). "Fled from Slavery, Dorchester County, Maryland, 1857." http://msa.maryland.gov/megafile/msa/speccol/sc5400/sc5496/007900/007978/html/007978bio.html

[52] Ibid.

In June, just a few weeks after Samuel Green's 1857 conviction, Harriet came to Poplar Neck in Caroline County to bring her parents north.

Ben Ross and Harriet Green

Dorchester County, Maryland

Earlier in 1854, Harriet had come back to the area to again help her brothers Ben and Henry (Harry), and this time Robert, to freedom. During Christmas, slave owners would often allow enslaved men and women to visit relatives if they were on nearby plantations; so this was a good time to escape.

Some time before Christmas, in 1854, Harriet got a friend of hers to write a letter to a man named Jacob Jackson. Jackson was a free black man who lived near the plantation where Ben, Henry and Robert were working as "hired" slaves. Jackson could read and write and he had an adopted son (William Henry Jackson), who was also free and who had moved up north. Harriet had her friend pretend that the letter was from Jacob's son, William. The coded message had various topics it in, but it also read:

> "Read my letter to the old folks, and give my love to them, and tell my brothers to be always watching unto prayer, and when the good old ship of Zion comes along, to be ready to step on board."
>
> Signed... "William Henry Jackson."[53]

Jacob Jackson was already under suspicion for helping "colored property" disappear from their owners. Therefore an inspector was used to read all of his mail before he was allowed to receive it. Jacob was called in and asked to read this letter from his adopted son because William Henry Jackson had no parents or brothers and the letter seemed suspicious. When Jacob read the letter, he threw it on the ground and said, "That letter can't be meant for me no how; I can't make head or tail

---

[53] Bradford, Sarah. *Harriet Tubman: The Moses of Her People.* 1886.

of it."

Jacob really knew what the letter meant... Harriet was coming soon and she wanted him to tell her brothers to be ready.

Harriet came the day before Christmas and sent word to her brothers to meet her at their father's cabin and to be ready to go. Others joined them, as well, and they gathered at Ben and Rit's cabin. Rit was expecting her sons to join her for Christmas and she had been cooking all day in preparation for their arrival. Harriet did not want her mother to see her, or her brothers, because she knew her mother would figure out what was going on and would "raise such an uproar" that the whole neighborhood might realize that they were getting ready to leave. So, she instructed them to hide in the fodder house. Harriet waited for everyone to arrive, while her mother waited around all day...looking for her sons to join her. Once all of the escapees got to the fodder house, Harriet sent two of them to her father's cabin...asking them to get Ben's attention, but not to notify her mother.

Ben came out of the cabin and figured out exactly what was going on. He immediately went back inside and got food and provisions for the group and made his way to the fodder house.

"I know what'll come of this, and I ain't gonna see my children, no how."

He held a handkerchief over his face, to cover up his eyes, and placed the food and clothing inside the door. He felt that if the authorities asked him whether he had seen his sons, he could honestly say, "No." Harriet then successfully led her brothers and the others to freedom…all the way to Canada.

Shores of the Choptank River, near Ben Ross' home.

That was the kind of man Ben Ross was, so in 1857, when Harriet suspected that her father might be implicated for helping the "Dover Eight," she made plans to come get her parents, right away.

Ben and Rit were not actually slaves at this time; Ben was freed after Anthony Thompson's death and he worked after that to earn enough money to buy Rit. Some time around 1855 (well after Edward Brodess' death), Ben paid Eliza Brodess $20 for his wife, Rit. Rit was over the age of forty-five and could, therefore, not be freed according to Maryland law. So, Ben purchased his wife and they lived together in Caroline County, Maryland while Ben worked for the timber operations of his former owner's son.

In June of 1857, Harriet came to rescue her father from any potential danger. This was no ordinary trip because both of her parents were in their seventies; going through wooded areas, navigating through wetlands, and traveling on foot would not be easy.

Harriet secured a makeshift wagon with a pair of "old wheels, a board on the axle to sit on," and another board that could swing, with ropes on it, "to rest their feet on." They made the trip all the way from the Eastern Shore of Maryland (using her resources, her networks and her intelligence) to St. Catharines, Canada.

Ben and Rit Ross joined several of their children in Canada, thanks to Harriet's efforts.

Chapter 7:

Harpers Ferry and Troy, NY

On October 16, 1859, at around 8:00 p.m., John Brown and his men launched their assault on the United States Armory and Arsenal in Harpers Ferry, Virginia. In a simultaneous action, a couple of Brown's men went to the home of two nearby slave owners, took them as hostages and freed men and women there who were enslaved.

So by midnight, two arsenal buildings were captured and two plantations had been raided, with those who were enslaved there freed. Hostages were held at the fire engine house (near the arsenals) and, by daylight, employees who were reporting for work were being taken as well.

By 7:00 a.m. locals began firing at John Brown's men and by 10:00 a.m. militia units had surrounded them. There were 21 men with John Brown; several of them were his sons. The raid was over soon after it began as militiamen and citizens stormed Brown and his men in their positions—freeing most of the hostages.

People began to crowd in the streets and by 11:00 p.m., Col. Robert E. Lee (who would become a famous general in the Confederate army) arrived with U.S. marines. By 7:00 a.m., the next morning, a party of marines stormed the engine house where John Brown and some of his men were still held up. All-in-all, of the 21 men who accompanied John Brown, 10 were killed, 5 escaped and 6 were captured...along with Brown. Brown was charged with conspiring with slaves to rebel, also with murder and treason against the state of Virginia. On December 2, 1859 he was hanged and all of the men, who were captured, were also tried and hanged.[54]

In April and May of 1858 (over a year before this famous raid) John Brown visited Canada hoping to get Harriet Tubman to support him in his efforts and seeking to recruit men from among the many black men who had escaped to Canada. Harriet Tubman did not end up (obviously) joining John Brown, but she did develop a deep admiration for him and he developed a great respect for her.

Wendell Phillips (a well-known abolitionist) recalled that the last time he saw John Brown was at his home and that Brown brought Harriet Tubman with him—referring to her as "General Tubman" and saying that she was one of the "bravest" people he knew.

---

[54] National Park Service. Harpers Ferry National Historic Park. "John Brown's Raid." "The Raiders."

Troy, NY in April 1860

About four months after the death of John Brown, Harriet Tubman was on her way to a women's suffrage meeting in Boston, when she decided to stop in Troy, New York to visit people she knew. Soon after she arrived, the town was in an uproar because of the capture of a man named Charles Nalle. Nalle had escaped from slavery in Virginia and made his way to Troy. His half brother, who was also his owner, was there in Troy to claim Nalle as his property, under the authority of the Fugitive Slave Act of 1850. Nalle was being held at the commissioner's office and as a crowd grew in front of the office, everyone tried to get a glimpse of what was happening.

African-American people were gathered across the street and white townspeople were directly in front of the building. People from the crowd began to yell out and someone offered to pay Nalle's owner $1,200. Then someone yelled, "$200 to the man who sets Charles free, and nothing to his owner!"

Harriet worked with the people who were organizing an attempt to free Nalle. She disguised herself as an old woman, tied a bonnet around her head, and made her way inside the building. The authorities noticed this "old lady" in the way and told her she had to leave the premises. She refused to go and pretended she didn't understand what they were saying. The time came for Charles to be taken down to see a judge a couple of blocks away, since his lawyer had filed a motion.

A wagon was in front of the building to carry him away and the authorities told the crowd that they would take him out of the front of the building, if everyone made a path and acted orderly.

Harriet began to move and the people, who were in on the plan, knew that Charles was about to come down because Harriet's bonnet was no longer visible in the window.

When the authorities left the building, they marched outside to a throng of people (well over one thousand) who were demanding that Charles Nalle be set free!

Charles' owner walked out, along with officers, and people were surprised to see how much Charles and his half-brother looked alike—they were both very light and looked similar.

Harriet made her way outside and knocked down one of the officers and tore away another. She then locked her arms in between Nalle's shackled arms, and around him, and didn't let go! There were many witnesses to this event and Martin Townsend, Nalle's lawyer, was one of them. He described Harriet's efforts:

> "...she was repeatedly beaten over the head with policemen's clubs, but she never for a moment released her hold, but cheered Nalle and his friends with her voice, and struggled with the officers until they were literally worn out with their exertions, and Nalle was separated from them.
>
> True, she had strong and earnest helpers in her struggle, some of whom had white faces..., and are now in Heaven. But she exposed herself to the fury of the sympathizers with slavery, without fear, and suffered their blows without flinching."[55][56]

---

[55] Bradford, Sarah. *Harriet Tubman: The Moses of Her People.* 1886.

[56] See also, Wilbur H. Siebert Collection. "Martin Ingham Townsend's letter to Wilbur Siebert, Sept. 4, 1896." Accessed February 2015.

The struggle went on for over 30 minutes. Harriet yelled to Charles' other rescuers, "Drag us out! Drag him to the river! Drown him! but don't let them have him!"

They went down to the river and Nalle was placed in a boat. There was also a ferry nearby to carry people across the river. Harriet separated from Nalle and another person took him across, while Harriet went on the ferry with the others.

When Nalle got to the other side, the authorities were waiting for him and they immediately took him. By the time Harriet and the others got to the other side Charles Nalle had been taken into a building. They found out where he had been taken and devised another plan, right on the spot.

A group of men and women (some of them were armed) gathered at the front of the building where Nalle was being held and stormed through the door. When they broke inside, the authorities fired at them. Two of the men who were at the front of the charge were shot and their bodies blocked the doorway. Harriet and some other women (who were armed) made it over the men's bodies and ran upstairs. They grabbed Nalle and took him back down the steps (over the men's bodies) and out of the door.

Some of the folks stopped the first man they saw in a wagon, who happened to be a black man, and asked him for his help. He knew the gravity of the situation and took Nalle, in his wagon, and off they went. Harriet left soon thereafter.

Charles Nalle was able to buy his freedom with the help of friends and later returned to Troy...a free man.

This event happened in Troy, New York on April 27, 1860, several months before what was most likely Harriet's final trip to rescue people from the Eastern Shore.

On that trip, in November of 1860, she rescued several people, including a man, his wife, their six-year-old daughter, their four-year-old daughter and their three-month-old infant.

Chapter 8:

From Questions of this Class Spring all Our Constitutional Controversies

The Lincoln Memorial, Washington, D.C.

In that same year, 1860, Abraham Lincoln was elected President of the United States on November 7, 1860. The very next month, on December 20, 1860, South Carolina seceded from the Union—then, Mississippi did so on January 9 1861; Florida on January 10, 1861; Alabama on January 11, 1861; Georgia on January 19, 1861; Louisiana on January 26, 1861; Texas on February 1, 1861; Virginia on April 17, 1861; Arkansas on May 6, 1861; North Carolina on May 20, 1861; and Tennessee on June 8, 1861.

When Lincoln took the oath of office the country was on the brink of war and seven states had already seceded from the United States. There are those who have argued that the war wasn't centrally about slavery, it was mostly about the rights of states, but that doesn't square with the words spoken at the time and the analysis of historical documents.

The constitutional controversies that were raging at that time were largely related to slavery and Lincoln says as much in his first inaugural address on March 4, 1861.

That morning Lincoln rose and met with outgoing President James Buchanan, and later he took the oath of office, which was administered to him by Chief Justice Roger B. Taney (the same Chief Justice who wrote the opinion in the Dred Scott case).[57]

Fellow-Citizens of the United States:

In compliance with a custom as old as the Government itself, I appear before you to address you briefly and to take in your presence the oath prescribed by the Constitution of the United States to be taken by the President "before he enters on the execution of this office."

---

[57] America's Library. "Abraham Lincoln's Inauguration." March 4, 1861.

I do not consider it necessary at present for me to discuss those matters of administration about which there is no special anxiety or excitement.

Apprehension seems to exist among the people of the Southern States that by the accession of a Republican Administration their property and their peace and personal security are to be endangered. There has never been any reasonable cause for such apprehension. Indeed, the most ample evidence to the contrary has all the while existed and been open to their inspection. It is found in nearly all the published speeches of him who now addresses you. I do but quote from one of those speeches when I declare that—

I have no purpose, directly or indirectly, to interfere with the institution of slavery in the States where it exists. I believe I have no lawful right to do so, and I have no inclination to do so.

Those who nominated and elected me did so with full knowledge that I had made this and many similar declarations and had never recanted them; and more than this, they placed in the platform for my acceptance, and as a law to themselves and to me, the clear and emphatic resolution which I now read:

Resolved, That the maintenance inviolate of the rights of the States, and especially the right of each State to order and control its own domestic institutions according to its own judgment exclusively, is essential to that balance of power on which the perfection and endurance of our political fabric depend; and we denounce the lawless invasion by armed force of the soil of any State or Territory, no matter what pretext, as among the gravest of crimes.

I now reiterate these sentiments, and in doing so I only press upon the public attention the most conclusive evidence of which the case is susceptible that the property, peace, and security of no section are to be in any wise endangered by the now incoming Administration. I add, too, that all the protection which, consistently with the Constitution and the laws, can be given will be cheerfully given to all the States when lawfully demanded, for whatever cause—as cheerfully to one section as to another.

There is much controversy about the delivering up of fugitives from service or labor. The clause I now read is as plainly written in the Constitution as any other of its provisions:

No person held to service or labor in one State, under the laws thereof, escaping into another, shall in consequence of any law or regulation therein be discharged from such service or labor, but shall be delivered up on claim of the party to whom such service or labor may be due.

It is scarcely questioned that this provision was intended by those who made it for the reclaiming of what we call fugitive slaves; and the intention of the lawgiver is the law. All members of Congress swear their support to the whole Constitution—to this provision as much as to any other. To the proposition, then, that slaves whose cases come within the terms of this clause 'shall be delivered up' their oaths are unanimous. Now, if they would make the effort in good temper, could they not with nearly equal unanimity frame and pass a law by means of which to keep good that unanimous oath?

There is some difference of opinion whether this clause should be enforced by national or by State authority, but surely that difference is not a very material one. If the slave is to be surrendered, it can be of but little consequence to him or to others by which authority it is done. And should anyone in any case be content that his oath shall go unkept on a merely unsubstantial controversy as to how it shall be kept?

Again: In any law upon this subject ought not all the safeguards of liberty known in civilized and humane jurisprudence to be introduced, so that a free man be not in any case surrendered as a slave? And might it not be well at the same time to provide by law for the enforcement of that clause in the Constitution which guarantees that "the citizens of each State shall be entitled to all privileges and immunities of citizens in the several States"?

I take the official oath to-day with no mental reservations and with no purpose to construe the Constitution or laws by any hypercritical rules; and while I do not choose now to specify particular acts of Congress as proper to be enforced, I do suggest that it will be much safer for all, both in official and private stations, to conform to and abide by all those acts which stand unrepealed than to violate any of them trusting to find impunity in having them held to be unconstitutional.

It is seventy-two years since the first inauguration of a President under our National Constitution. During that period fifteen different and greatly distinguished citizens have in succession administered the executive branch of the Government. They have conducted it through many perils, and generally with great success. Yet, with all this scope of precedent, I now enter upon the same task for the brief constitutional term of four years under great and peculiar difficulty. A disruption of the Federal Union, heretofore only menaced, is now formidably attempted.

I hold that in contemplation of universal law and of the Constitution the Union of these States is perpetual. Perpetuity is implied, if not expressed, in the fundamental law of all national governments. It is safe to assert that no government proper ever had a provision in its organic law for its own termination. Continue to execute all the express provisions of our National Constitution, and the Union will endure forever, it being impossible to destroy it except by some action not provided for in the instrument itself.

Again: If the United States be not a

government proper, but an association of States in the nature of contract merely, can it, as a contract, be peaceably unmade by less than all the parties who made it? One party to a contract may violate it—break it, so to speak—but does it not require all to lawfully rescind it?

Descending from these general principles, we find the proposition that in legal contemplation the Union is perpetual confirmed by the history of the Union itself. The Union is much older than the Constitution. It was formed, in fact, by the Articles of Association in 1774. It was matured and continued by the Declaration of Independence in 1776. It was further matured, and the faith of all the then thirteen States expressly plighted and engaged that it should be perpetual, by the Articles of Confederation in 1778. And finally, in 1787, one of the declared objects for ordaining and establishing the Constitution was "to form a more perfect Union."

But if destruction of the Union by one or by a part only of the States be lawfully possible, the Union is less perfect than before the Constitution, having lost the vital element of perpetuity.

It follows from these views that no State upon its own mere motion can lawfully get out of the Union; that resolves and ordinances to that effect are legally void, and that acts of violence within any State or States against the authority of the United States are insurrectionary or revolutionary, according to circumstances.

I therefore consider that in view of the Constitution and the laws the Union is unbroken, and to the extent of my ability, I shall take care, as the Constitution itself expressly enjoins upon me, that the laws of the Union be faithfully executed in all the States. Doing this I deem to be only a simple duty on my part, and I shall perform it so far as practicable unless my rightful masters, the American people, shall withhold the requisite means or in some authoritative manner direct the contrary. I trust this will not be regarded as a menace, but only as the declared purpose of the Union that it will constitutionally defend and maintain itself.

In doing this there needs to be no bloodshed or violence, and there shall be none unless it be forced upon the national authority. The power confided to me will be used to hold, occupy, and possess the property and places belonging to the Government and to collect the duties and imposts; but beyond what may be necessary for these objects, there will be no invasion, no using of force against or among the people anywhere. Where hostility to the United States in any interior locality shall be so great and universal as to prevent competent resident citizens from holding the Federal offices, there will be no attempt to force obnoxious strangers among the people for that object. While the strict legal right may exist in the

Government to enforce the exercise of these offices, the attempt to do so would be so irritating and so nearly impracticable withal that I deem it better to forego for the time the uses of such offices.

The mails, unless repelled, will continue to be furnished in all parts of the Union. So far as possible the people everywhere shall have that sense of perfect security which is most favorable to calm thought and reflection. The course here indicated will be followed unless current events and experience shall show a modification or change to be proper, and in every case and exigency my best discretion will be exercised, according to circumstances actually existing and with a view and a hope of a peaceful solution of the national troubles and the restoration of fraternal sympathies and affections.

That there are persons in one section or another who seek to destroy the Union at all events and are glad of any pretext to do it I will neither affirm nor deny; but if there be such, I need address no word to them. To those, however, who really love the Union may I not speak?

Before entering upon so grave a matter as the destruction of our national fabric, with all its benefits, its memories, and its hopes, would it not be wise to ascertain precisely why we do it? Will you hazard so desperate a step while there is any possibility that any portion of the ills you fly from have no real existence? Will you, while the certain ills you fly to are greater than all the real ones you fly from, will you risk the commission of so fearful a mistake?

All profess to be content in the Union if all constitutional rights can be maintained. Is it true, then, that any right plainly written in the Constitution has been denied? I think not. Happily, the human mind is so constituted that no party can reach to the audacity of doing this. Think, if you can, of a single instance in which a plainly written provision of the Constitution has ever been denied. If by the mere force of numbers a majority should deprive a minority of any clearly written constitutional right, it might in a moral point of view justify revolution; certainly would if such right were a vital one. But such is not our case. All the vital rights of minorities and of individuals are so plainly assured to them by affirmations and negations, guaranties and prohibitions, in the Constitution that controversies never arise concerning them. But no organic law can ever be framed with a provision specifically applicable to every question which may occur in practical administration. No foresight can anticipate nor any document of reasonable length contain express provisions for all possible questions. Shall fugitives from labor be surrendered by national or by State authority? The Constitution does not expressly say. May Congress prohibit slavery in the Territories? The Constitution does not expressly say. Must Congress protect slavery in the

Territories? The Constitution does not expressly say.

From questions of this class spring all our constitutional controversies, and we divide upon them into majorities and minorities. If the minority will not acquiesce, the majority must, or the Government must cease. There is no other alternative, for continuing the Government is acquiescence on one side or the other. If a minority in such case will secede rather than acquiesce, they make a precedent which in turn will divide and ruin them, for a minority of their own will secede from them whenever a majority refuses to be controlled by such minority. For instance, why may not any portion of a new confederacy a year or two hence arbitrarily secede again, precisely as portions of the present Union now claim to secede from it? All who cherish disunion sentiments are now being educated to the exact temper of doing this.

Is there such perfect identity of interests among the States to compose a new union as to produce harmony only and prevent renewed secession?

Plainly the central idea of secession is the essence of anarchy. A majority held in restraint by constitutional checks and limitations, and always changing easily with deliberate changes of popular opinions and sentiments, is the only true sovereign of a free people. Whoever rejects it does of necessity fly to anarchy or to despotism. Unanimity is impossible. The rule of a minority, as a permanent arrangement, is wholly inadmissible; so that, rejecting the majority principle, anarchy or despotism in some form is all that is left.

I do not forget the position assumed by some that constitutional questions are to be decided by the Supreme Court, nor do I deny that such decisions must be binding in any case upon the parties to a suit as to the object of that suit, while they are also entitled to very high respect and consideration in all parallel cases by all other departments of the Government. And while it is obviously possible that such decision may be erroneous in any given case, still the evil effect following it, being limited to that particular case, with the chance that it may be overruled and never become a precedent for other cases, can better be borne than could the evils of a different practice. At the same time, the candid citizen must confess that if the policy of the Government upon vital questions affecting the whole people is to be irrevocably fixed by decisions of the Supreme Court, the instant they are made in ordinary litigation between parties in personal actions the people will have ceased to be their own rulers, having to that extent practically resigned their Government into the hands of that eminent tribunal. Nor is there in this view any assault upon the court or the judges. It is a duty from which they may not shrink to decide cases properly brought before them, and it is no fault of theirs if others seek to turn their decisions to political purposes.

One section of our country believes slavery is right and ought to be extended, while the other believes it is wrong and ought not to be extended. This is the only substantial dispute. The fugitive-slave clause of the Constitution and the law for the suppression of the foreign slave trade are each as well enforced, perhaps, as any law can ever be in a community where the moral sense of the people imperfectly supports the law itself. The great body of the people abide by the dry legal obligation in both cases, and a few break over in each. This, I think, can not be perfectly cured, and it would be worse in both cases after the separation of the sections than before. The foreign slave trade, now imperfectly suppressed, would be ultimately revived without restriction in one section, while fugitive slaves, now only partially surrendered, would not be surrendered at all by the other.

Physically speaking, we can not separate. We can not remove our respective sections from each other nor build an impassable wall between them. A husband and wife may be divorced and go out of the presence and beyond the reach of each other, but the different parts of our country can not do this. They can not but remain face to face, and intercourse, either amicable or hostile, must continue between them. Is it possible, then, to make that intercourse more advantageous or more satisfactory after separation than before? Can aliens make treaties easier than friends can make laws? Can treaties be more faithfully enforced between aliens than laws can among friends? Suppose you go to war, you can not fight always; and when, after much loss on both sides and no gain on either, you cease fighting, the identical old questions, as to terms of intercourse, are again upon you.

This country, with its institutions, belongs to the people who inhabit it. Whenever they shall grow weary of the existing

Government, they can exercise their constitutional right of amending it or their revolutionary right to dismember or overthrow it. I can not be ignorant of the fact that many worthy and patriotic citizens are desirous of having the National Constitution amended. While I make no recommendation of amendments, I fully recognize the rightful authority of the people over the whole subject, to be exercised in either of the modes prescribed in the instrument itself; and I should, under existing circumstances, favor rather than oppose a fair opportunity being afforded the people to act upon it. I will venture to add that to me the convention mode seems preferable, in that it allows amendments to originate with the people themselves, instead of only permitting them to take or reject propositions originated by others, not especially chosen for the purpose, and which might not be precisely such as they would wish to either accept or refuse. I understand a proposed amendment to the

Constitution—which amendment, however, I have not seen—has passed Congress, to the effect that the Federal Government shall never interfere with the domestic institutions of the States, including that of persons held to service. To avoid misconstruction of what I have said, I depart from my purpose not to speak of particular amendments so far as to say that, holding such a provision to now be implied constitutional law, I have no objection to its being made express and irrevocable.

The Chief Magistrate derives all his authority from the people, and they have referred none upon him to fix terms for the separation of the States. The people themselves can do this if also they choose, but the Executive as such has nothing to do with it. His duty is to administer the present Government as it came to his hands and to transmit it unimpaired by him to his successor.

Why should there not be a patient confidence in the ultimate justice of the people? Is there any better or equal hope in the world? In our present differences, is either party without faith of being in the right? If the Almighty Ruler of Nations, with His eternal truth and justice, be on your side of the North, or on yours of the South, that truth and that justice will surely prevail by the judgment of this great tribunal of the American people.

By the frame of the Government under which we live this same people have wisely given their public servants but little power for mischief, and have with equal wisdom provided for the return of that little to their own hands at very short intervals. While the people retain their virtue and vigilance no Administration by any extreme of wickedness or folly can very seriously injure the Government in the short space of four years.

My countrymen, one and all, think calmly and well upon this whole subject. Nothing valuable can be lost by taking time. If there be an object to hurry any of you in hot haste to a step which you would never take deliberately, that object will be frustrated by taking time; but no good object can be frustrated by it. Such of you as are now dissatisfied still have the old Constitution unimpaired, and, on the sensitive point, the laws of your own framing under it; while the new Administration will have no immediate power, if it would, to change either. If it were admitted that you who are dissatisfied hold the right side in the dispute, there still is no single good reason for precipitate action. Intelligence, patriotism, Christianity, and a firm reliance on Him who has never yet forsaken this favored land are still competent to adjust in the best way all our present difficulty.

In your hands, my dissatisfied fellow-countrymen, and not in mine, is the momentous issue of civil war. The Government will not assail you. You can have no conflict without being yourselves the aggressors. You have no oath registered in heaven to destroy the

Government, while I shall have the most solemn one to "preserve, protect, and defend it."

I am loath to close. We are not enemies, but friends. We must not be enemies. Though passion may have strained it must not break our bonds of affection. The mystic chords of memory, stretching from every battlefield and patriot grave to every living heart and hearthstone all over this broad land, will yet swell the chorus of the Union, when again touched, as surely they will be, by the better angels of our nature.[58]

—Abraham Lincoln: 1st Inaugural Address, March 4, 1861

---

[58] Joint Congressional Committee on Inaugural Ceremonies. The 19th Presidential Inauguration: Abraham Lincoln, March 4, 1861. Accessed November 2016. http://www.inaugural.senate.gov/about/past-inaugural-ceremonies/19th-inaugural-ceremonies

While there was much discussion about whether or how a state should secede and the manner in which states could administer their own institutions without oversight and interference from the federal government, those issues, at the time, were clearly related to the issue of slavery. Lincoln accurately summed it up when he said,

> "Shall fugitives from labor be surrendered by national or by State authority? The Constitution does not expressly say. May Congress prohibit slavery in the Territories? The Constitution does not expressly say. Must Congress protect slavery in the Territories? The Constitution does not expressly say.
>
> From questions of this class spring all our constitutional controversies,…"

Later he states,

> "One section of our country believes slavery is right and ought to be extended, while the other believes it is wrong and ought not to be extended. This is the only substantial dispute."

Of course there was another section of the country that believed that slavery should never have been instituted in the first place.

Chapter 9:

Gullah Islands, Intelligence and the Civil War

On April 12, 1861 Confederate forces fired on Fort Sumter, in Charleston, South Carolina. Union troops surrendered the fort some thirty-four hours later...and the Civil War had officially begun.

Just over a month later, General Benjamin Butler (a Union general) took command of Fort Monroe in Virginia. Soon after the arrival of Butler, three African-American men showed up at Fort Monroe. They had been enslaved by a Confederate colonel who intended to send them to North Carolina; to force them to help Confederate forces there. These three men decided that they were not going to be enslaved anymore and they escaped.

Union commanders were not given any special instructions, at first, about what to do with enslaved men and women if they made their way to Union forts and to areas under Union control. Some commanders sent them back, others put them to work, etc.

General Butler, thus, had to decide what he would do. That same day Virginia voters approved the ordinance to secede from the Union, so Virginia was technically a foreign country. When a representative of the men's owner rode to Fort Monroe, under a white flag, and demanded that the three men be sent back under the authority of the Fugitive Slave Act and the Constitution, General Butler refused.

Butler reasoned that he had no obligation to fulfill these requests for a foreign country, which Virginia was claiming to be and that since these enslaved men were technically property and were going to be used in efforts against the United States, he could seize them and not allow them to be returned.

The decision of these men (and others like them) to take their freedom into their own hands was the first forceful step in making the military leaders of the war face up to the realities on the ground—enslaved men and women were going to take courageous steps to ensure their freedom and they were going to bring along valuable information when they did so.

Black 'Dispatches"— Intelligence

Of the hundreds of thousands of African Americans who left slavery and made their way to Union encampments throughout the course of the war, many also participated in activities that brought important details to Union commanders and supported military expeditions.

For example, in May of 1862 William Jackson crossed into Union lines. Jackson was the personal coachman of Jefferson Davis, the former U. S. senator and now the Confederate president. William Jackson heard Davis speak of specific plans and he dared to share that information directly with Union military forces. Whatever the information was, because there are no remaining records of what he reported, it was immediately sent by General McDowell, to the War Department, in Washington, D.C.[59]

---

[59] Central Intelligence Agency. "Black Dispatches: Black American Contributions to Union Intelligence During the Civil War." Accessed 1-2016.

On another occasion, Mary Touvestre was a free (formerly enslaved) housekeeper of a Confederate engineer, during the Civil War. Before the war, the U.S. Navy had a significant naval base in Norfolk, VA. When the war began, the military ordered the destruction of ships in that base, so that they wouldn't fall into enemy hands.

Not all of the ships, however, were completely destroyed and Confederate forces were able to salvage enough of the USS Merrimack to begin rebuilding that ship. The plan was to turn the Merrimack into the first Confederate ironclad.

An ironclad was a ship outfitted with iron and steel, which made it easier for the ship to ram a wooden ship and it obviously also made it more difficult for an ironclad to be destroyed.

At the time, the United States had set up a blockade that prevented much needed supplies from getting to cities like Richmond and Norfolk.

Mary Touvestre worked for one of the engineers who was refurbishing the Merrimack into the ironclad, the Virginia. She overheard him talk about the ironclad and realized what that might mean. If the ironclad was successful, it could ram through the wooden ships of the Union blockade and allow needed supplies to be brought through.

This engineer brought a copy of the ship's plans home with him. Mary Touvestre took a copy of his plans and courageously brought them to Washington, D.C. This was a dangerous trip of espionage—a black woman carrying secret Confederate blueprints and plans to Washington, by way of Virginia. She did it, despite the obvious danger she faced.

It is unclear how she made it, but when she arrived in D.C., she asked for a meeting with the Department of Navy. They looked at her plans and heard what she described about the progress of the ship. Officials then decided to speed up the construction of their own ironclad (which was already underway, but not nearly as far along), the USS Monitor.[60]

In what became one of the most famous naval battles of the Civil War the Virginia and the USS Monitor met in combat.

---

[60] Central Intelligence Agency. Intelligence in the Civil War. Public Affairs, Central Intellegence Agency: Washington, D.C., 2007. https://www.cia.gov/library/publications/intelligence-history/civil-war/Intel_in_the_CW1.pdf

On March 8, 1862 the Virginia (the Confederate ship) launched a surprise attack on several U.S. ships. In just under an hour it sank the USS Cumberland and later damaged the USS Congress. It then attacked the USS Minnesota before stopping the assault, due to darkness.

That night, March 8th, the USS Monitor arrived and sailed into place. At about 7:30 am, when the battle ensued, the Monitor went out to meet the Virginia as it came back to finish off the Minnesota.

The two ships met and for hours they fired upon each other...neither one doing enough damage to sink the other. The battle ended in a draw and the Virginia was not able to break the Union blockade. This battle, called the "Battle of Hampton Roads," was the first time two ironclad ships met in such a contest and it paved the way for the construction of iron ships for use in war.

Mary Touvestre's remarkable courage was an important part of this historical event.

The feats and daring expeditions of some of these men and women were simply heroic and one such additional man should be remembered, as the war hero he was.

Robert Smalls was born in Beaufort, South Carolina on April 5, 1839. By the time the war came he was still enslaved and working in Charleston, South Carolina. Smalls had gained considerable skills in working with ships and, on May 13, 1862, an opportunity arose for him. He and other men were forced to work onboard the Planter. The Planter was a ship used to transport ammunitions around the area and on the night of

May 13th the white crew members went into town…leaving Smalls and the other enslaved men onboard—they had already discussed their plan.

Smalls put on the captain's hat and coat and the other men got the boat ready to sail. At about 2:00 am the Planter set out and the men, including Smalls, were able to get their wives and children onboard. Smalls knew how to pilot the ship, so he correctly navigated the waters around Charleston. The danger was that they had to pass by several gun batteries, including Fort Sumter, to get to the Union ships that were blockading Charleston.

Smalls, by putting on the captain's attire, hid his face and when they passed each gun battery he gave the appropriate signal…which was returned, as the Confederate soldiers had no reason to think there was anything amiss. The ship was flying the Confederate flag and it sailed right out of Charleston's harbor.

As the Planter approached the first Union ships, it lowered the Confederate flag and raised a white flag. The Union officers discovered what was going on and Robert Smalls safely delivered the Confederate ship, along with all its ammunition, into Union hands. Smalls also began to help the Union by telling them where explosive devices were placed in the harbor and along the shores near Charleston...Smalls had actually been forced to place some of the explosives himself.

Smalls went on to pilot some ships for the Union and, after the war, he returned to Beaufort and became a member of the House of Representatives for South Carolina and later a member of the state Senate. In 1874 Smalls was elected to the U.S. House of Representatives and he served in the 44th, 45th, 47th, 48th and 49th U.S. Congresses.[61]

Robert Smalls, William Jackson and Mary Touvestre are examples of the kind of intelligence that was offered by African Americans as they sought their own freedom and encountered Union forces throughout the duration of the war. It became a practice to interview them as they came to Union encampments and the stream of information that came from them came to be known as "Black Dispatches."

---

[61] United State House of Representatives. History, Art & Archives. Smalls, Robert. Accessed November 2016. http://history.house.gov/People/Detail/21764

The Gullah Corridor

In the two years leading up to the Civil War (in 1859), Harriet moved herself, and her parents, to Auburn, New York. There she was among friends and abolitionists. In 1862, Governor John Albion Andrew, of Massachusetts, asked Harriet Tubman to participate in the war.

Governor Andrew felt that someone with her skills would be of great use to the United States.[62] Harriet, although she was caring for her elderly parents, decided to go. In May of 1862 (during the same month Robert Smalls made his daring escape), she went to Beaufort, South Carolina (not far from Hilton Head), which was the area where the headquarters of the Department of the South was located. To give you some idea of what this area was like, let's take a quick look at the history of an island like Hilton Head just before, and during, the Civil War.

This area of South Carolina is a part of the National Gullah Geechee Cultural Heritage Corridor.[63] This corridor stretches from

---

[62] Bradford, Sarah. *Harriet Tubman: The Moses of Her People.* 1886.

[63] Gullah Geechee Cultural Heritage Corridor. Our History and Culture. Accessed 11-2015. http://gullahgeecheecorridor.org

Wilmington, North Carolina to Florida's Jacksonville area. Hilton Head, Beaufort, and Port Royal are situated in the southeast corner of South Carolina and are about 80 - 90 miles south of Charleston.

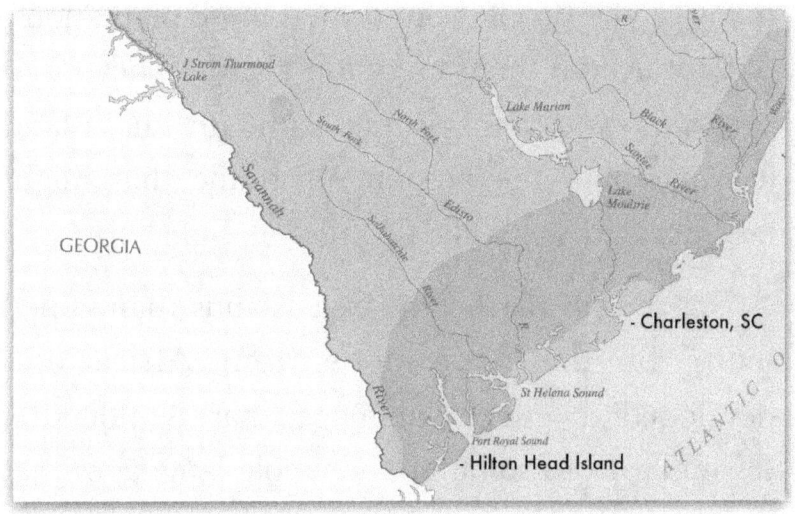

Hilton Head, today, is known for its beautiful beaches and is a major attraction, for tourists, in South Carolina.

Just prior to the Civil War, Hilton Head consisted of about 20 working plantations—mostly populated by enslaved men and women. The Gullah people, as you may know, were forced to come to the United States from rice-growing areas in Africa specifically for their skills in growing rice...as rice, cotton and indigo were the main crops in the lowland areas along the southeast coast of the U.S.

Because of the isolation of the sea islands along the coast of South Carolina, Georgia, Northern Florida and some parts of North Carolina...the people who were forced into slavery there developed their own distinct culture. In fact many of the people who owned those plantations, did not live on them in Hilton Head. They hired overseers and few visitors came to the island (compared to the amount of traffic that might take place in a city like Charleston, SC).

So, the people on the Sea Islands maintained many of their traditions from Africa and developed a creole language that is not that dissimilar from some of the creole languages that developed in Haiti and in Jamaica (and some of the other nations of the Caribbean). They continued their tradition of making baskets from the grass that grew around marshes and some of the words that have been introduced into the English language, from Africa, are attributed to the Gullah people.

Early during the Civil War, the Union decided to blockade Confederate cities to prevent supplies from coming in from Europe. In November of 1861, Union forces launched an attack along the northern border of Hilton Head Island near Port Royal Sound. Within hours, the main fort on the island had been surrendered and Union forces gained control over an important area that would become their base for blockading other areas in the South. Beaufort and St. Helena Island also fell a short time after.

Thousands of enslaved men and women were freed in the areas of Beaufort, Hilton Head, and St. Helena, as plantation owners (and their families) fled the area.

By December of 1861, there were hundreds of emancipated people in the Union encampment at Hilton Head and many more were about to make their way to the camp.

General Ormsby Mitchel ordered a village to be built that would house the increasing number of formerly enslaved people and the town of Mitchelville was born. There was a military supervisor appointed for the town, but the people of Mitchelville constructed their own homes and established their own government.

They elected a city council and created laws, or ordinances. Taxes were collected, as the people worked to support Union forces and were hired to do many tasks. The town also established sanitary regulations, punished violations of its ordinances, compensated its municipal officials and established a way to settle property and other disputes. In short, they performed all of the governmental and administrative tasks needed to run a town that grew to hold more than 3,000 people.

The people of Mitchelville also created and administered the first compulsory education law in South Carolina, which required that all of their children attend school on a daily basis. These were remarkable achievements given the fact that they were all subject to the horrors of slavery, only a short time earlier.

When Harriet Tubman came to South Carolina during the Civil War, she spent much of her time in Beaufort (about 30 miles north of Hilton Head), in Hilton Head and in other areas that are a part of the Gullah/Geechee Corridor.

Her service can best be summed up by a letter, written by General Rufus Saxton, after the war in support of her receiving a pension for her work:

From General Saxton to a Lady in Auburn.

March 21, 1868,

MY DEAR MADAME:

I have received your letter informing me that Hon. Wm. H. Seward, Secretary of State, would present a petition to Congress for a pension for Harriet Tubman, for services rendered in the Union Army during the late war. I can bear witness to the value of her service in South Carolina and Florida.

She was employed in the hospitals and as a spy. She made many a raid inside enemy's lines, displaying remarkable courage, zeal, and fidelity. She was employed by General Hunter, and I think by Generals Stevens and Sherman...

I am very truly yours,

RUFUS SAXTON, Bvt. Brig. Gen., U.S.A.

By the time the Civil War ended some 180,000 African Americans served in the Union Army; 18,000 in the Navy; thousands and thousands left their places of enslavement; and an untold number of African-American men and women provided intelligence, spied for, and supported the United States military—Harriet Tubman was one of these remarkable people.

Chapter 10:

The First Woman in American Military History

Harriet Tubman, as mentioned in General Saxton's letter, made "many a raid inside enemy lines." Her expertise in traveling undetected through difficult terrain proved useful in several military expeditions during the Civil War.

In June of 1863, one such raid took place. Harriet commanded a team of scouts who were charged with going into the areas surrounding the Combahee River, in South Carolina, to scout out the location of explosive devices that were designed to blow up invading Union ships and to determine where enemy defenses were stationed.

Some of the escaped slaves from the area and African-American volunteers were among those working with her to gather this information. Harriet originally developed the idea for this raid and was first asked to lead the raid herself, but she insisted that Colonel James Montgomery be in command. Col. Montgomery was a veteran of anti-slavery fighting in Kansas and was an associate of John Brown, whom as you know, Harriet also knew. In a report to Secretary of War Edwin Stanton, General Rufus Saxton said,

> "This is the only military command in American history wherein a woman, black or white, led the raid, and under whose inspiration, it was originated and conducted."[64]

---

[64] Central Intelligence Agency. "Intelligence in the Civil War: Black Dispatches." Accessed 2013.

This was remarkable, when you think about it. Here was a woman strategically planning and executing a military expedition in the 1800s. Historical accounts point to her skills as a scout, and to her strategic thought process, as being invaluable to this expedition.

Sometime before the raid actually happened, Confederate lookouts and soldiers (pickets) stationed along the Combahee River sounded a false alarm about what they believed was an invasion.

So, on June 2, 1863, when Union boats did come up the river, Confederate lookouts did not immediately notify others. Based on the intelligence gathered by Harriet and her team, and on her strategic direction, Union forces executed their plans.

Two Union gunboats made their way some twenty-five miles up the Combahee River; successfully navigating around the explosive devices that were designed to damage their boats and disembarking at several locations. As the ships sailed slowly up the river, African-American soldiers landed and went ashore. They encountered Confederate forces that were scattered all along the river, but were successfully able to overcome these defenses.

The soldiers waved flags and sounded horns to help alert slaves that they were there to free them, then proceeded to several strategic locations to destroy Confederate supplies and capture enemy assets.

They met very little resistance as the raid was well-planned and well-executed. Plantation owners watched as soldiers disembarked the gunboats and made their way to the plantations.

Slaves, who were told to fear Union soldiers, quickly got word that they were there to save them —not to harm them. Many slaves left their work, right in the middle of doing it, and ran toward the ships.

Harriet said she had never seen such a sight, as hundreds of people ran away from their places of bondage.

"Here you'd see a woman with a pail on her head, rice...smoking in it just as she'd taken it from the fire, young one hanging on behind,…"

Union soldiers waited at the shores aboard smaller canoes, to take the freed men, women and children to the Union boats. Harriet helped to calm people down as they rushed to get in the canoes, ensuring them that there was enough room for everybody on the boats.

Plantation homes were burned, crops were destroyed, Confederate supplies were obtained, and several warehouses were decimated. The raid was a complete success. All-in-all, over 700 men, women and children were freed from slavery that day and not one soldier from the Second South Carolina Volunteers was lost.

As Caregiver

As we have mentioned, Harriet spent time in what is now called the Gullah Geechee Cultural Heritage Corridor, while she was in South Carolina. It is unclear exactly whom she met while there, but it is clear that Gullah people, with their unique heritage, were all throughout this area.

She described her reaction upon meeting some of the formerly enslaved people of this area.

> "Why, their language down there in the far South is just as different from ours in Maryland as you can think.
>
> They laughed when they heard me talk, and I could not understand them, no how."

This may have been a reference to the type of creole language that Gullah people developed on the Sea Islands.

Harriet Tubman also described a funeral she attended on Hilton Head Island. The funeral was held at midnight because during slavery there they were not allowed to bury their dead during the day and they continued that custom during this time on the island. The men and women stood around with pine torches in their hands to light up the area as the body was placed in the middle of their circle.

The preacher began to preach and the people began to sing. Harriet recalled, "I wish you could hear them sing… There voices are so sweet."

The preacher reminded the attendees that no one could escape death. "You can't go to that big fort (pointing to a fort on Hilton Head) and shut yourself up there… but death will find you there."

After the sermon, all of the congregation then went around in a dance and a song, shaking each person's hand…reminding them that they too were bound to go. Harriet participated in the funeral, but she was not known to everyone there, so when they came around to her (instead of calling her name) they simply said, "Everybody's bound to go!"[65]

The attendees then carried their pine torches in a procession to the designated burial place of the deceased person.

---

[65] Bradford, Sarah. *Harriet Tubman: The Moses of Her People.* 1886.

Harriet further described some of her experiences in the hospitals, as she spent a good deal of time, when she was not on spying expeditions, caring for colored soldiers in hospitals.

> "I'd go to the hospital...early every morning. I'd get a big chunk of ice, ..., and put it in a basin, and fill it with water; then I'd take a sponge and begin. First man I'd come to, I'd thrash away the flies, and they'd rise, ..., like bees around a hive. Then I'd begin to bathe their wounds,..."

Harriet was not paid, regularly, for her services while with the Union Army (she received about $200 during her time of service), so she baked pies, made gingerbread and made her own root beer. She then hired others to sell the food and drinks she made in the camps.

In Beaufort, South Carolina, she took some of the money she earned and built a wash house for the women in the camp there so that they could have a decent facility within which to wash clothes and earn money based on the work they did around the area.

During her time in South Carolina she was also called away to Fernandina (in Florida) to take care of soldiers who were "dying off like sheep" from dysentery.[66]

She used the roots and herbs which grew near the waters and made medicinal solutions which proved to be effective for many of the people who were suffering from the disease.

Harriet later took a leave of absence, where she visited her parents and travelled in New England. Her stay was longer than expected (she may have become ill) and she had to obtain another pass to travel via government transport back to South Carolina.[67] On her way back, she was stopped by women (nurses) who told her of the atrocities in the hospitals for colored soldiers in Fort Monroe, Virginia (the same Fort Monroe where General Butler made his famous decision not to return people into the hands of slaveholders).

Harriet changed her plans and went to the area around Fort Monroe in Hampton, VA. After

---

[66] Ibid.

[67] Conrad, Earl. "Charles P. Wood Manuscripts of Harriet Tubman." *Negro History Bulletin*, January 1, 1950.

staying there for several months (and traveling to highlight the conditions of black soldiers in the hospitals there), Harriet Tubman's service in the Civil War ended.

After Harriet Tubman ended her time in the war, she travelled back to New York to her home in Auburn. During her journey she was questioned by a conductor onboard a train. The conductor did not believe she had the right to sit in the seat she was occupying, although Harriet told him she was traveling via government transport which allowed her to sit in her seat.

The conductor told her, "We don't carry niggers for half-fare."

Harriet refused to get out of her seat and the conductor tried to forcibly remove her. During the struggle, Harriet called him a "scoundrel" and he began to choke her. She also told him that she didn't thank anybody to call her a colored person —that she would rather he called her "black" or "Negro" and that she was just as proud of being black as he was of being white.[68]

The conductor continued to try to get her out of her seat, but he was not able to do it on his own. So, he called two additional men to help him. The three men pried her fingers from what she was holding on to and aggressively wrenched her arm—the violent struggle took place in front of the other passengers, as some of them cheered them on and yelled for the men to throw her off the train.

They grabbed her and threw her into the smoking car and Harriet Tubman suffered broken bones and serious injuries as a result.

---

[68] McGowan, James A. and William C. Kashatus. *Harriet Tubman: A Biography.* Santa Barbara: Greenwood, 2011.

212

Chapter 11:

We're Rooted

As we have mentioned, Harriet Tubman purchased a home from William H. Seward (who would become Secretary of State under Abraham Lincoln), for very favorable terms. Harriet had gotten to know many people through her travels and her freedom-fighting activities brought her into contact with some of the most committed abolitionists of her time.

Her travels brought her to places like Boston, where she met with people who knew of her efforts and she began to speak in several anti-slavery events.

In the summer of 1859, supporters of the Massachusetts Anti-Slavery Society gathered for a Fourth of July event to recommit themselves to the fight against slavery. Thomas Wentworth Higginson served as president of this event. He was an avid abolitionist and a supporter of John Brown; he would also become a commander, in the Civil War, of the First South Carolina Volunteers, a regiment of black men in the same area of South Carolina where Harriet went during the Civil War.[69]

During the event Higginson introduced Harriet Tubman to the crowd. Tubman had come to the area to raise money for the home which she had purchased from William H. Seward, with the hope that she could support her

---

[69] Higginson, Thomas W. (1823 - 1911). *Army Life in a Black Regiment.* First published in 1869. Reprinted, Riverside Press, 1900.

family in her new home. The anti-slavery newspaper, *The Liberator,* covered the event and noted Harriet's speech in this way (she was introduced as "Moses," so as not to give away her identity as this was 1859):

> "'Moses,' the deliverer, stood up before the audience, who greeted her with enthusiastic cheers. She spoke briefly, telling the story of her sufferings as a slave, her escape, and her achievements on the Underground Railroad, in a style of quaint simplicity, which excited the most profound interest in her hearers. The mere words could do no justice to the speaker, and therefore we do not undertake to give them; but we advise all our readers to take the earliest opportunity to see and hear her."

The crowd raised a collection of thirty-seven dollars, for which Harriet thanked them.[70]

Harriet also spoke at the Convention of

---

[70] Yerrinton, Jas. M.W. "The Fourth at Framingham." *The Liberator.* July 8, 1859.

Colored Citizens of New England, the very next month, in August of 1859.

The convention was held to discuss ways to elevate the black population of the country given the assaults on their human rights by the Fugitive Slave Act (1850) and the Supreme Court's Dred Scott decision. The issue of emigration to Africa came up during the convention and was a topic of heated debate.

George Thomas Downing

George Thomas Downing (of Rhode Island) was elected president of the convention. Downing was a prominent businessman who opened up restaurants and a luxury hotel in Rhode Island. He famously participated in protests against the capture of Anthony Burns (he reportedly ripped a sign from police officers who had taken that sign from a group of protestors) in

Massachusetts in 1854 and, in 1857, he helped to spearhead efforts to desegregate school systems in Rhode Island.

George Downing was an opponent of colonization and he made his feelings known, vehemently, during the convention.

Of course the topic of colonization was not new. There were those who saw the growing numbers of free African Americans in society as a problem and who did not have as their goal the immediate abolition of slavery such as the American Colonization Society (which had prominent members like Senator Henry Clay—the "Great Compromiser"; Francis Scott Key—author of the *Star Spangled Banner;* President James Madison; and Bushrod Washington—Associate Justice of the Supreme Court).

There were, however, blacks who supported the idea of colonization and part of the reason for the heated discussion at this particular convention was that, during the previous year, the African Civilization Society was formed by the well-known African-American minister, Henry Highland Garnet. Supporters of the African Civilization Society were present at this convention in New England, where Harriet Tubman was in attendance, in 1859.

She rose to the podium on the second day of this convention and made her thoughts on the topic of colonization known to the audience.

She was introduced as one of the most successful conductors on the Underground Railroad and her last name was changed...most likely to conceal her identity.

She told the story of a man who planted garlic and onions (which are potent crops) in his land, hoping that it would increase his dairy production, but he soon found that it made his butter too strong and therefore he wasn't able to sell it in the markets. He then decided to plant clovers instead, but he found that the wind had blown the garlic and onions all over his farm. Just like this man, she said, white people had gotten black people to do their drudgery and now they wanted to root them out. "But," she said, "**they can't do it; we're rooted here, and they can't pull us up**."[71]

---

[71] "New England Colored Citizens' Convention." *The Liberator.* August 26, 1859.

Harriet Tubman 1822(?) - 1913

Appendix:

Final Thoughts

Harriet Tubman's first husband died in Maryland and Harriet remarried. She met and married Nelson Davis, who was himself also a Civil War veteran, and they were married for almost twenty years, until his death in 1888.

People who knew Harriet often said that she frequently had men and women whom she took care of, in her home, despite not being able to provide for herself or her family, at times. That was a consistent "fault" that many people who knew her observed. Harriet Tubman lived a life of sacrifice and of service to others:

- she personally went into slave territory to rescue dozens upon dozens of people from enslavement;
- she gave information and guidance to many other people which led to their successful escapes;
- she responded, in a moment's notice, to

help free people she didn't even know, such as Charles Nalle in Troy, NY;

- she supported, though she did not join, John Brown's efforts to spark a rebellion amongst the enslaved people in Virginia;

- she served in the Civil War and became the first American woman to lead a strategic military expedition and raid in American history (freeing over 700 men, women and children in one such raid);

- on February 28, 1899, **"An Act Granting an Increase in Pension to Harriet Tubman Davis"** was passed by the U.S. Congress (not for her own service in the war, but as the widow of Nelson Davis);

- she also consistently opened her home to people in need, in Auburn, during the later part of her life;

- and she worked to establish a home for elderly African Americans in Auburn, NY, before her death.

She died in Auburn, NY on March 10, 1913, after having lived for over ninety years.

References and Photos by Chapter

CHAPTER 1: THE BACKDROP FOR HER LIFE

Danish National Archives. "The Danish Slave Trade—Timeline for Teaching Purposes," Rigsarkivet. Accessed 8-2016.

Eltis, David. "A Brief Overview of the Trans-Atlantic Slave Trade." Voyages: The Trans-Atlantic Slave Trade Database. Accessed May 3, 2016. http://www.slavevoyages.org/assessment/essays#

General Services Administration: The African Burial Ground. "GSA and the African Burial Ground." Accessed April 2015.

Hebrard, Jean. "Slavery in Brazil: Brazilian Scholars in the Key Interpretive Debates." University of Michigan Center for Latin and Caribbean Studies. Vol. 1, 2013.

National Archives and Records Administration. "Teaching with Documents: Eli Whitney's Patent for the Cotton Gin." Accessed May 2015.

New York Historical Society. "Slavery in New York." Accessed April 2015. http://www.slaveryinnewyork.org/history.htm.

Northup, Solomon. *Twelve Years a Slave: Narrative of Solomon Northup, a Citizen of New York, Kidnapped in Washington City in 1841, and Rescued in 1853, from a Cotton Plantation Near the Red River, in Louisiana.* Auburn: Derby & Miller, 1853.

Reuters. "In-Depth, Chronology: Who banned slavery when? March 22, 2007." http://www.reuters.com/article/uk-slavery-idUSL1561464920070322

U.S. Department of State, Office of the Historian. "Milestones 1801-1829: Louisiana Purchase, 1803." Accessed Nov. 2016. https://history.state.gov/milestones/1801-1829/louisiana-purchase

Williams, Arden. "Catharine Greene (1755 - 1814)." *New Georgia Encyclopedia.* Georgia Humanities Council. Accessed May 2015.

PHOTOS:

Harriet Tubman, full-length portrait, standing with hands on back of a chair, Lindsley, H. B., photographer. Created/Published: between ca. 1860 and 1875, Library of Congress LC-USZ62-7816

View of the World, United States Geological Survey, The National Map.

New York City, 2014, Red and Black Ink, LLC.

Lower Manhattan, 2010, Red and Black Ink, LLC.

CHAPTER 2: SOCIAL AND MORAL/RELIGIOUS SUPPORT FOR SLAVERY

"Anthony Burns in New York", "Ransom of Burns". *The Liberator.* Garrison, William Lloyd, March 9, 1855.

Boston Slave Riot and the Trial of Anthony Burns. Boston: Fetridge and Company, 1854. http://memory.loc.gov/cgi-bin/query/r?ammem/llstbib:@field(NUMBER+@band(llst+019))

Douglass, Frederick. *My Bondage and My Freedom.* 1855.

Joint Special Committee of the Senate and House of Representatives of the State of Massachusetts on the Petition of George Latimer and Others. House, No. 41, Commonwealth of Massachusetts, General Court, 1843, pp. 1, 2, 36, 37. https://archive.org/details/commonwealthofma00adam
National Park Service. 'New Bedford Whaling National Historical Park: Leonard Grimes." Accessed February 24, 2015.

PBS Online. "Africans in America: Anthony Burns Captured." Accessed October 2015. www.pbs.org/wgbh/aia/part4/4p2915.html

Richardson, James Daniel. *A Compilation of the Messages and Papers of the Confederacy.* Nashville: United States Publishing Company, 1905, pg. 68.

St. Catharines Museum, Museum Chat. "Salem Chapel, BME Church and Zion Baptist Church." February 9, 2016. https://stcatharinesmuseumblog.com/2016/02/09/salem-chapel-bme-church-and-zion-baptist-church/. Accessed September 28, 2016.

Stevens, Charles Emery. *Anthony Burns: A History.* Boston: John P. Jewett and Company, 1856.

U.S. Congressional Documents and Debates, 1774 - 1875, *Congressional Globe*, Senate, 36th Congress, 2nd Session, pg. 487.

PHOTOS:

Frederick Douglass, Frederick Douglass National Historic Site, FRDO 3928

Anthony Burns / drawn by Barry from a daguereotype [sic] by Whipple & Black ; John Andrews, engraver. Boston : R.M. Edwards, printer, c1855.

National Park Service. Leonard Grimes. Men of Mark: Eminent, Progressive and Rising, 1887.

CHAPTER 3: POLITICAL ACTIONS THAT SUPPORTED THE EXISTENCE OF SLAVERY

A Century of Lawmaking for a New Nation: U.S. Congressional Documents and Debates, 1774 - 1875. *Register of Debates*, Senate, 24th Congress, 1st Session. Pages 765, 766, & 777. https://memory.loc.gov/cgi-bin/ampage?collId=llrd&fileName=022/llrd022.db&recNum=386

Library of Congress: Primary Documents in American History. "Compromise of 1850." https://www.loc.gov/rr/program/bib/ourdocs/Compromise1850.html

Library of Congress. Primary Documents in American History. "Dred Scott v. John F. A. Sanford."

Library of Congress. Primary Documents in American History. "Missouri Compromise."

National Archives and Records Administration. "Struggles over Slavery: The 'Gag' Rule." Accessed February 2016. http://www.archives.gov/exhibits/treasures_of_congress/text/page10_text.html

OurDocuments.gov. "Transcript of Missouri Compromise (1820)." Accessed May 2016.

Ourdocuments.gov U.S. National Archives and Records Administration. Kansas-Nebraska Act. Accessed May 2016.

Sumner, Charles. *The Crime Against Kansas: Speech of Hon. Charles Sumner in the Senate of the United States, 19th and 20th May, 1856*. Boston: John P. Jewett and Co., 1856.

United States Senate. Senate History. "1851 - 1877: May 22, 1856, The Caning of Senator Charles Sumner." Accessed May 2016. http://www.senate.gov/artandhistory/history/minute/The_Caning_of_Senator_Charles_Sumner.htm

U.S. Capitol Visitor Center. "The Gag Rule." https://www.visitthecapitol.gov/exhibitions/more-perfect-union-april-2012-september-2012/freedom/gag-rule

PHOTOS:

Capitol Building, 2012, Red and Black Ink, LLC.

California Road, 2013, Red and Black Ink, LLC.

Supreme Court Building, 2015, Red and Black Ink, LLC.

Harriet Tubman, full-length portrait, standing with hands on back of a chair, Lindsley, H. B., photographer. Created/Published: between ca. 1860 and 1875, Library of Congress LC-USZ62-7816

CHAPTER 4: THE PLACE WHERE HARRIET TUBMAN WAS BORN

Bradford, Sarah. *Harriet Tubman: The Moses of Her People.* 1886.

Braford, Sarah. *Scenes in the Life of Harriet Tubman.* Auburn: W. J. Moses, Printer, 1869.

Douglass, Frederick. *My Bondage and My Freedom.* 1855.

Harriet Tubman Underground Byway. "Finding a Way to Freedom: Dorchester and Caroline Counties, Driving Tour." http://harriettubmanbyway.org.

Larson, Kate Clifford. *Bound for the Promise Land.* New York: Ballantine Books, 2004.

Maryland State Archives. MSA SC 5496-8445. Archives of Maryland (Biographical Series). Benjamin Ross (b. circa 1787 - d. 1871). "Accomplice to slave flight, Caroline County, Maryland, 1857." Accessed September 2013. http://msa.maryland.gov/megafile/msa/speccol/sc5400/sc5496/008400/008445/html/008445bio.html

McGowan, James A. and William C. Kashatus. *Harriet Tubman: A Biography.* Santa Barbara: Greenwood, 2011.

PHOTOS:

Great Blue Heron, Dorchester County, 2015, Red and Black Ink, LLC.

Map of Dorchester, Talbot and Caroline Counties, Red and Black Ink, LLC.

Douglass Chesapeake Bay, 2013, Red and Black Ink, LLC.

Talbot County Forest, 2013, Red and Black Ink, LLC.

The Marker in Dorchester, Maryland Civil War Centennial Commission.

Wetlands in the Eastern Shore, 2013, Red and Black Ink, LLC.

Choptank River, 2013, Red and Black Ink, LLC.

Wildlife Refuge, Dorchester County, 2015, Red and Black Ink, LLC.

Wildlife, Dorchester County, 2015, Red and Black Ink, LLC.

Map of Choptank River, Red and Black Ink, LLC.

Scene from the Area Near Harriet Tubman's Home, 2013, Red and Black Ink, LLC.

CHAPTER 5: SOLEMN RESOLUTION

Adkins Arboretum. A walking tour. Nature's Role in the Story of the Underground Railroad. http://www.adkinsarboretum.org/programs_events/ugrr.html

Bradford, Sarah. *Harriet Tubman: The Moses of Her People.* 1886.

Braford, Sarah. *Scenes in the Life of Harriet Tubman.* Auburn: W. J. Moses, Printer, 1869.

Larson, Kate Clifford. *Bound for the Promise Land.* New York: Ballantine Books, 2004.

Maryland State Archives, MSA SC 5496-1535. Josiah "Joe" Bailey (b. 1828 - d. ?). "Fled from slavery, Talbot County, Maryland, 1856." Accessed September 2013.

National Underground Railroad, Network to Freedom. "Kessiah's Flight." Historical marker.

Still, William. *The Underground Railroad: A Record of Facts, Authentic Narratives, Letters, etc.* (Philadelphia: Porter & Coates, 1872), pp. 272-274.

PHOTOS:

Harriet Tubman, full-length portrait, standing with hands on back of a chair, Lindsley, H. B., photographer. Created/Published: between ca. 1860 and 1875, Library of Congress LC-USZ62-7816

Talbot County Forest, Again, 2013, Red and Black Ink, LLC.

Forest Floor— 2013, Talbot County, Red and Black Ink, LLC.

Green Growth on Side of Tree, 2013, Red and Black Ink, LLC.

Map of Choptank River, Red and Black Ink, LLC.

Choptank River at Sunset, 2013, Red and Black Ink, LLC.

Banks of the Choptank Near Ben Ross's Home, 2013, Red and Black Ink, LLC.

Snow-Covered Ground, Eastern Shore, 2016, Red and Black Ink, LLC.

Moon in Maryland, 2015, Red and Black Ink, LLC.

Dorchester County Circuit Court House, 2015, Red and Black Ink, LLC.

Shores of the Choptank River, 2013, Red and Black Ink, LLC.

Niagara Falls, 2013, Red and Black Ink, LLC.

CHAPTER 6: HARRIET'S PARENTS, OTHER HEROES AND THE DOVER EIGHT

Bradford, Sarah. *Harriet Tubman: The Moses of Her People.* 1886.

Maryland State Archives. MSA SC 5496-7978. Henry Predeaux (b. circa 1830 - d. ?). "Fled from Slavery, Dorchester County, Maryland, 1857." http://msa.maryland.gov/megafile/msa/speccol/sc5400/sc5496/007900/007978/html/007978bio.html

Maryland State Archives, MSA SC 3520-13785. Samuel Green (b. 1802 - d. 1877). "Arrested for possession of Uncle Tom's Cabin, Dorchester County, 1857, Alleged accomplice to slave flight, 1854 - 1857." http://msa.maryland.gov/megafile/msa/speccol/sc3500/sc3520/013700/013785/html/13785bio.html

Still, William. *The Underground Railroad: A Record of Facts, Authentic Narratives, Letters, etc.* Philadelphia: Porter & Coates, 1872.

PHOTOS:

The Root, 2015, Red and Black Ink, LLC.

Samuel Green, ("Ten Years in the Penitentiary for Having a Copy of Uncle Tom's Cabin"). Still, William. *The Underground Railroad: A Record of Facts, Authentic Narratives, Letters, etc.* Philadelphia: Porter & Coates, 1872.

Scene from Dorchester County, 2015, Red and Black Ink, LLC.

Choptank River, Poplar Neck, Near the Home of Ben Ross, 2013, Red and Black Ink, LLC.

Niagara Falls, 2013, Red and Black Ink, LLC.

CHAPTER 7: HARPERS FERRY AND TROY, NY

Bradford, Sarah. *Harriet Tubman: The Moses of Her People.* 1886.

National Park Service. Harpers Ferry National Historic Park. "John Brown's Raid." "The Raiders."

Wilbur H. Siebert Collection. "Martin Ingham Townsend's letter to Wilbur Siebert, Sept. 4, 1896." Accessed February 2015.

PHOTOS:

Harpers Ferry Historic Park Area, 2015, Red and Black Ink, LLC.

CHAPTER 8: FROM QUESTIONS OF THIS CLASS SPRING ALL OUR CONSTITUTIONAL CONTROVERSIES

America's Library. "Abraham Lincoln's Inauguration." March 4, 1861.

Joint Congressional Committee on Inaugural Ceremonies. The 19th Presidential Inauguration: Abraham Lincoln, March 4, 1861. Accessed November 2016. http://www.inaugural.senate.gov/about/past-inaugural-ceremonies/19th-inaugural-ceremonies

PHOTOS:

The Lincoln Memorial, 2015, Red and Black Ink, LLC.

Up Close Memorial, 2015, Red and Black Ink, LLC.

CHAPTER 9: GULLAH ISLANDS, INTELLIGENCE AND THE CIVIL WAR

Bradford, Sarah. *Harriet Tubman: The Moses of Her People.* 1886.

Central Intelligence Agency. "Black Dispatches: Black American Contributions to Union Intelligence During the Civil War." Accessed 1-2016.

Central Intelligence Agency. Intelligence in the Civil War. Public Affairs, Central Intellegence Agency: Washington, D.C., 2007. https://www.cia.gov/library/publications/intelligence-history/civil-war/Intel_in_the_CW1.pdf

CWSAC Battle Summaries: Hampton Roads. The American Battlefield Protection Program. Accessed 1-2016. http://www.nps.gov/abpp/battles/va008.htm

Finding Freedom's Home: Archaeology at Mitchelville. Accessed 11-2015. http://www.bcgov.net/mitchelville/

Gullah Geechee Cultural Heritage Corridor. Our History and Culture. Accessed 11-2015. http://gullahgeecheecorridor.org

Library of Congress. "Abraham Lincoln Papers at the Library of Congress: The Emancipation Proclamation." https://www.loc.gov/teachers/classroommaterials/connections/abraham-lincoln-papers/history6.html

National Park Service. "Major General Benjamin F. Butler." Fort Monroe National Park.

NOAA. Battle of Hampton Roads. "USS Monitor: Preserving a Legacy." National Ocean Service. Accessed January 2016. http://monitor.noaa.gov/150th/hampton.html

Town of Hilton Head. History of Hilton Head Island. "The Civil War and Union Occupation." http://www.hiltonheadislandsc.gov/ourisland/history.cfm?menuheader=1

United State House of Representatives. History, Art & Archives. Smalls, Robert. Accessed November 2016. http://history.house.gov/People/Detail/21764

PHOTOS:

Antietam National Battlefield, 2015, Red and Black Ink, LLC.

Gettysburg Cannon, 2016, Red and Black Ink, LLC.

Cannon, 2016, Red and Black Ink, LLC.

Landscape, 2016, Red and Black Ink, LLC.

Cannon Back, 2016, Red and Black Ink, LLC.

Map of South Carolina, Red and Black Ink, LLC.

CHAPTER 10: THE FIRST WOMAN IN AMERICAN MILITARY HISTORY

Bradford, Sarah. *Harriet Tubman: The Moses of Her People.* 1886.

Central Intelligence Agency. "Intelligence in the Civil War: Black Dispatches." Accessed 2013.

Conrad, Earl. "Charles P. Wood Manuscripts of Harriet Tubman." *Negro History Bulletin,* January 1, 1950.

Conrad, Earl. General Tubman. Campaign on the Combahee. The Commonwealth, a Boston Newspaper. http://www.harriettubman.com/tubman2.html

McGowan, James A. and William C. Kashatus. *Harriet Tubman: A Biography.* Santa Barbara: Greenwood, 2011.

Official Records of the War of the Rebellion. Series 1, vol xiv. page 307. United States War Dept., John Sheldon, et al. Government Printing Office, Washington, DC, 1885. http://ebooks.library.cornell.edu/m/moawar/text/waro0020.txt Cornell

U.S. National Archives and Records Administration. Legislative Branch. "Congress and Harriet Tubman's Claim for a Pension (Congress in History)." Accessed https://www.archives.gov/legislative/resources/education/tubman

- General affidavit of Harriet Tubman relating to her claim for a pension, ca. 1898; Records of the U.S. House of Representatives, National Archives Identifier 306573.

- Letter from Sereno E. Payne, on behalf of the claim of Harriet Tubman that she was employed as a nurse, cook, and a spy, February 5, 1898; Records of the U.S. House of Representatives, National Archives Identifier 306574.

- H.R. 4982, a bill granting a pension to Harriet Tubman Davis, late a nurse in the U.S. Army, January 19, 1899; Records of the U.S. House of Representatives, National Archives Identifier 306578. Transcript

- S. Rpt. 1619 to accompany a bill granting a pension to Harriet Tubman Davis, February 7, 1899; Records of the U.S. House of Representatives, National Archives Identifier 7330232.

- An Act Granting and Increase in Pension to Harriet Tubman Davis, February 28, 1899; 30 Stat 1539, Records of the General Government.

PHOTOS:

Cannon, 2016, Red and Black Ink, LLC.

Cannon Back, 2016, Red and Black Ink, LLC.

Train Tracks, 2015, Red and Black Ink, LLC.

CHAPTER 11: WE'RE ROOTED

Bradford, Sarah. *Harriet Tubman: The Moses of Her People.* 1886.

Higginson, Thomas W. (1823 - 1911). *Army Life in a Black Regiment.* First published in 1869. Reprinted, Riverside Press, 1900.

Library of Congress. American Memory. Today in History: July 26. The American Colonization Society." Accessed February 2016. https://memory.loc.gov/ammem/today/jul26.html

Library of Congress. Slaves and the Courts, 1740-1860, A part of a speech pronounced by Francis S. Key, Esq. on the trial of Reuben Crandall, M.D. : before the Circuit court of the District of Columbia, at the March term thereof, 1836, on an indictment for publishing libels with intent to excite sedition and insurrection among the slaves and free coloured people of said district. https://memory.loc.gov/cgi-bin/ampage?collId=lst_rbcmisc&fileName=lst/lst0099//rbcmisclst0099.db&recNum=2&itemLink=D%3Fllstbib%3A1%3A.%2Ftemp%2F%7Eammem_isMC%3A%3A&linkText=0

"New England Colored Citizens' Convention." *The Liberator.* August 26, 1859.

Washington, S. A. M. *George Thomas Downing; sketch of his life and times.* Newport: The Milne Printery, 1910.

"Woman's Rights Convention." The Liberator. July, 6 1860.

Yerrinton, Jas. M.W. "The Fourth at Framingham." *The Liberator.* July 8, 1859.

PHOTOS:

Harriet Tubman, full-length portrait, seated in chair, facing front, probably at her home in Auburn, New York. Date Created/Published: [1911], Reproduction Number: Library of Congress, LC-DIG-ppmsca-02909

Washington, S. A. M. *George Thomas Downing; sketch of his life and times.* Newport: The Milne Printery, 1910.

1895 portrait of Harriet Tubman, courtesy Harriet Tubman Underground Railroad National Monument.

VISIT US AT OUR WEBSITE FOR MORE TITLES

BlackandEducation.com

www.ingramcontent.com/pod-product-compliance
Lightning Source LLC
LaVergne TN
LVHW051516070426
835507LV00023B/3147